aha!

aha!

POINTS OF LIGHT

life defining moments

JUDI AND DAN CUMMING : EDITORS

© Copyright 2004 Danaca Investments Inc. All rights reserved.

No part of this publication may be reproduced, stored in a retrieval system, or transmitted, in any form or by any means, electronic, mechanical, photocopying, recording, or otherwise, without the written prior permission from Judi Cumming, president, Danca Investments Inc., owner of the copyright.
Email: momentseditor@hotmail.com.

Printed in Victoria, Canada

Cover and graphics by Danielle Krysa

A cataloguing record for this book that includes the U.S. Library of Congress Classification number, the Library of Congress Call number and the Dewey Decimal cataloguing code is available from the National Library of Canada. The complete cataloguing record can be obtained from the National Library's online database at: www.nlc-bnc.ca/amicus/index-e.html
ISBN: 1-4120-1753-X

TRAFFORD

This book was published *on-demand* in cooperation with Trafford Publishing. On-demand publishing is a unique process and service of making a book available for retail sale to the public taking advantage of on-demand manufacturing and Internet marketing. **On-demand publishing** includes promotions, retail sales, manufacturing, order fulfilment, accounting and collecting royalties on behalf of the author.

Suite 6E, 2333 Government St., Victoria, B.C. V8T 4P4, CANADA
Phone   250-383-6864   Toll-free   1-888-232-4444 (Canada & US)
Fax   250-383-6804   E-mail   sales@trafford.com
Web site   www.trafford.com   TRAFFORD PUBLISHING IS A DIVISION OF TRAFFORD HOLDINGS LTD.
Trafford Catalogue #03-2130   www.trafford.com/robots/03-2130.html

10   9   8   7   6   5   4   3   2

Prologue

When I look back at my life, it is the moments I remember - those moments that sparkle with insight and liberation or cut with a lesson waiting to be learned. One day I found myself reflecting on the understanding and wisdom that had clicked into place for me through these 'points of light' and decided to write them down, starting from my childhood. No sooner would I finish one, than another would come to mind.

I began to wonder about other people's 'aha!' experiences and decided to ask my family and friends if they wanted to share theirs. Although I was living in Malaysia at the time, the miracle of email allowed for easy communication.

I was thrilled as the responses filled my inbox – episodes of transformation ranging from the simple to the sublime from so many friends and family members living in Canada and abroad. My 87-year-old aunt, Mary Coderre is the eldest of the contributors and Neil Chantler, a 23-year-old classmate of my son, the youngest. The universal quality of these flashes of insight was amazing – I could identify with them easily and profoundly.

My call for requests was to only a small circle of friends and family who have email and yet, among them, they have shared enough life defining moments to fill the pages of this book! I cannot help but think that this is only the tip of the Moments Iceberg.

Our hope is that sharing our instants of illumination will motivate you to remember yours and together we'll turn these points of light into a beacon of inspiration. If you have a Moment you would like to share, please email momentseditor@hotmail.com to request submission guidelines.

Judi Cumming

Acknowledgments

    We want to express love and gratitude to all the contributors whose willingness to share important, personal experiences allowed this book to happen. Very few of them are professional writers, but the power and genuineness of their accounts is undeniable.

    Special thanks to our daughter Danielle Krysa, a talented multimedia designer, for making this book look good. Thanks also to Elsie Neufeld whose editing expertise helped enormously to get this project off the ground.

"Sooner or later we all discover the important moments in life are not the advertised ones, not the birthdays, the graduations, the weddings, not the great goals achieved. The real milestones are less prepossessing. They come to the door of memory."

- Susan B. Anthony

CONTENTS

INSPIRATION

Faceted Memories ... 11
    Margaret Coderre-Williams
A Moment a Day ... 14
    Pam Boucher
A Joyful Noise ... 15
    Larry Coderre
Last Catch ... 17
    Jeffrey S. Oxford
He Loves Me Anyway ... 20
    Judi Cumming
Mariah of Milwaukee ... 22
    Mary Elizabeth Looby
Running on Empty ... 24
    Judy Miller
Finding My Voice ... 26
    N. M. Coderre/S. Emery
Sufficient Grace ... 28
    Mary Coderre

CONNECTION

My Father who art in Heaven ... 31
    Dave Coderre
Katie's Gift ... 33
    Kathy Bissett
Guardians of Land and Sea ... 35
    Margot Wawra
A Father's Gift ... 37
    Dan Cumming
Threads of Ancestry ... 39
    Stephen Emery
Burnt Offerings ... 40
    Marika Kohut

Nine to One ... 42
    Cynthia Lee-Strawford
Blowing in the Wind ... 44
    Allison Stokholm

FREEDOM

The Last Taboo ... 47
    Anonymous
Round Trip? ... 49
    Danielle Krysa
Border Run ... 51
    Neil Chantler
Choices ... 54
    Janna Cumming
Of Death and Thanksgiving ... 55
    Judi Cumming
Peace and Joy ... 56
    Marika Kohut
Monica, Mother and Me ... 58
    Judi Cumming
Out of the Blue! ... 60
    Terry Boucher
Warmth on a Wintry Day ... 62
    Kathy Bissett

AHA!

Is the Latte Frothier on the Other Side? ... 64
    Danielle Krysa
Sixty Year Moment ... 66
    Mary Coderre
Collaborative Trust ... 68
    Susan Nelson
Holding Him ... 69
    Margaret Coderre-Williams
Nothing is Real ... 71
    Judi Cumming

Napoleon WAS Here! ... 72
    Kathy Bissett
My Little Farmer ... 73
    Lucille Ranger
Highway to Heaven? ... 75
    Gregory Krysa
Timeless Mindless ... 78
    Cameron Cumming
My Guardian Angel with Quills ... 80
    Margot Wawra

INSIGHT

Washtub ... 83
    Larry Coderre
Man the Protector ... 86
    Margot Wawra
Demons ... 88
    Judi Cumming
Anxiety ... 90
    Pat Coderre
Internal Youth ... 91
    Margot Wawra
A Moment of Truth ... 92
    Bill Coderre
When to Say Goodbye ... 95
    Barbara Purdy
Don't Ask Why ... 96
    Gina Hartley
September 11: Hard Lesson in Priorities ... 98
    Dave Watson
My New Coat ... 101
    Anita Coderre
The Empty Room ... 103
    Cynthia Lee-Strawford

ONENESS

Insight into Light ... 106
    Kate Miller
The Birthday Yogi ... 107
    Judi Cumming
I Belong to the Earth ... 109
    Catherine Poupard
The Kiss ... 110
    Judi Cumming
Going for the 'Gold' ... 111
    Dan Cumming
Love, Dad ... 114
    Olwyn Irving

INDEX OF AUTHORS ... 116

INSPIRATION

My children had given me an ornament as a birthday present - it was metallic and leaf-shaped, with several small crystal prisms incorporated into it. Wanting to put it where it would catch the light, I hung it on a window in the stairwell to the second floor of my house. Every sunny day, when I walked through the stairwell, I was greeted by a wondrous profusion of soft-tinted rainbows. This day, my eyes were drawn back to the prisms themselves. Marveling at how the faceted surfaces could capture and refract light, I imagined, for a moment, memories being captured and refracted in the same way - memories of my father, who had died only a few months before.
This poem flowed from that moment:

Faceted Memories

I view life now
through the prism of my father's death.
Through faceted memories,
tinted with sadness -
the time-softened remnant of grief.
Through rhythms too.
Filtered lyrics and refrains.
Echos of the many songs
I know my father liked.

They were an eclectic mix.
Sentimental favourites
sharing equal place
with soul-searing solos.
Joined, on rare occasion,
by story-woven songs -
but only those whose endings
had an unexpected twist.
Try To Remember,
the September song of enduring love,
and the poignant Killing Me Softly,
unexpectedly side by side

with the one-hit-wonder
The Night That The Lights Went Out In Georgia

I hear those songs, and others now,
not with my own ears but, as if, with his.
Listening for lyrics with the complex simplicity,
or simple complexity,
that so intrigued him.

Don't It Make My Brown Eyes Blue

Often he would share such songs with me.
Or with the collective me - my family.
Sharing first, last, and always,
his pleasure in the words.
The music being secondary, a vehicle only,
for the clever twists of meaning
in the words.

Words. His words.
Joking. Provoking.
His precious gift.
My fondest memory.
And now, it would seem,
my release.

I see him,
seldom but sometimes,
in my dreams.
In such a dream, a recent one,
the words of a song eluded me.
And then he was there,
say-singing the words -
a refrain that I've forgotten since.
Remembering instead
the enduring image
of the man.

My father.

Smiling.
Eyes, blue and crystal-bright,
chiding me a little, perhaps -
for my obvious surprise at seeing him.

Saying,
without any need of words,
how could I ever think that he was gone?

Margaret Coderre-Williams
Orleans Ontario

A Moment a Day

For most of my life and especially since retirement when I have had time to enjoy a quieter lifestyle, I have enjoyed moments in which I contemplate the beauty of life. I think of these as my special memories and try to find one each day to remember.

It can be something in nature which moves me such as the song of a bird, a beautiful butterfly, a perfect bloom or a sunset. Sometimes it is an interaction with strangers, perhaps a shy smile from a passing child. Or it can be something more family-based such as a phone call from one of my children or a quiet moment with my husband.

Many of my moments have taken place at our cottage, probably because that is where I have always found the peace I relish - the call of a loon breaking the silence of a moonlit night, extended family grouped around a campfire roasting marshmallows, mist rising from the water in the early morning.

Recent years have brought a change in our lives. My husband and I are living in Southeast Asia and my moments have changed. Now they tend to be memories of the exotic swirl of life in which we find ourselves - the Cambodian sun setting over Angkor Wat, a woman wearing a beautiful sari in a teeming street in India, Malaysian children playing in the rain during a monsoon deluge.

What makes these memories so special is that I have learned to savour them when they happen and remember them in my "memory of the day" collection. Usually I think of these at night, often before falling asleep but any quiet, peaceful time in the day is a good time for me to reflect. It is usually a brief interlude but it brings me contentment and appreciation for every day that passes.

Pam Boucher   Subang Jaya, Malaysia

A Joyful Noise

Congregational singing is a Protestant thing. That is what most Catholics thought as the 1950's drew to a close. While our Separated Brethren were belting out 'Bringing in the Sheaves' and 'Amazing Grace', in their churches, we were sitting, kneeling and standing in silence in ours, watching the priest and altar boys pray with their backs to us and listening to the choir sing behind us. At least we were all facing in the same direction. But, all that was about to change.

A new Pope was elected that year and he took the name John. He summoned the Catholic bishops to Rome to reexamine the Church. Over a period of four years this Council, known as Vatican II, promulgated 16 documents initiating radical changes within the Church. Many thought that the most radical was the one suggesting that the laity should actually pray with the priest and sing with the choir at Mass.

To facilitate this participation, the altar was moved so that the priest could stand behind it facing the assembly and the prayers were translated into the vernacular. In some parishes the transition went well. In our parish, however, there was a great deal of confusion and although we had begun to respond feebly to the prayers, singing seemed out of the question because our choir had evaporated.

Fortunately, there were other forces at work. While the Pope and bishops were pouring down all these documents making wholesale changes to the Church, little movements were percolating up through the grass roots changing the Church one soul at a time. Such a movement, which began in Spain, was the *Cursillo*, the 'Little Course'. Its purpose was to gather laymen together in small groups to learn more about their Faith and the new ways of seeing and celebrating it. These 'Little Courses' were so successful that the idea soon leaped across the Atlantic, first to Latin America and from there, into the United States and Canada. By this time the *Cursillo* had developed into weekend retreats, one for men and one for women.

  A good friend, who was among the few from our parish who had made a *Cursillo*, invited me to attend one. There was an indefinable urgency in his invitation that compelled me to accept it. Another member of our parish was there too. Because he had a good, powerful voice and we had no musical accompaniment, he was asked to lead the singing at Mass and at other times. Celebrating Mass in this way was a new and joyful experience for most of us as we all joined in the prayers and hymns.

  Monday evening, the day after the retreat, I had a strong desire to go to our parish Mass. About a half dozen *Cursillistas* were there, including our 'lead singer'. When the priest entered the sanctuary in silence, our new *Cursillista* began to sing the entrance hymn we had learned. All the others who knew the hymn joined in the singing. We also sang at the other parts of the Mass. It seemed so right! It was all very spontaneous but I felt, and I am sure the others did too, that we were following a director whose hands could be seen only by our hearts.

  The following Sunday, we sang at Mass. We made up in enthusiasm what we lacked in talent. That enthusiasm proved contagious because after a few weeks and bit of encouragement, members of the congregation began to sing with us.

  A new choir was born of our offerings, that first night after our return from *Cursillo*. And for me, although the whole thing took some time to gain momentum, it was all summed up that Monday night when, at the end of Mass, our pastor looked at us and said, "Miracles still happen".

Larry Coderre   Ottawa ON

Last Catch

The last year of high school was wrapping up for me as the remnants of the winter were melting away. School seemed to be more work than the part-time job I held at McDonald's. I worked because I wanted a car of my own - what teenager didn't want the same! I enjoyed driving and yearned for the freedom my own car would give me - even if that freedom was only imagined.

I didn't see my dad a lot that spring, usually only long enough for him to give me the keys to the family car. My dad has always been a hard worker, at home, in his career and as a father. As a sergeant with 20 years experience in the Air Force, he had to work very hard. He was always trying to instill in me that work ethic but I am not sure he was completely successful. Our family was not rich by any means but my father made sure we always had a roof over our heads and food enough to eat. Both my brother and I looked up to and were proud of him.

One night I did not have to work so I was downstairs watching television in our family room. When my dad walked in through the front door, I called up to him from my place on the couch. He asked how school was and then went into his bedroom to change. Since my brother would not be home until after his football practice, I would have to find out when supper would be ready. I finished watching TV and went upstairs to the kitchen. I was chased out with my hand still hurting and my mom still swinging the spoon – so much for my attempt to steal a meatball! It would be another half an hour until supper.

That was just enough time, I thought to myself. I called up to Dad and picked up the ball and gloves from the hallway chair where they had been left from the last game of catch, and waited outside for him.

My dad seemed a little off for some reason; he was throwing the ball wildly and dropping the baseball more times than I had seen in my entire life. He seemed to be getting a little upset after every bad throw. Something was irritating him; I hoped it wasn't something I was doing. I chased after another badly thrown ball that had bounced into the ditch. By the time I managed to retrieve the ball from the mud and the tall grass, my dad was gone. Only the sound of the slamming front door echoed his leaving. I looked down the empty street where we had been playing catch only to see a well used baseball glove lying on the spot were my father had just stood. My thoughts were confused. Questions filled my brain. I bent down to retrieve my father's glove, wondering what I might have done to cause such a reaction in him.

My mother was waiting for me as I walked through the front door and into the hall.

"Where is Dad?" I asked. No answer was given.

"We need to talk, Dear," was her only response.

My mother took my arm as we walked to the kitchen table. I felt the weight of her body increase with every step. By the time we reached the table I felt as if I carried both of us. My heart was racing and my mind spinning as I sat down in my chair. I still held the baseball gloves and ball in my arms, which seemed to give me comfort that I had never felt nor ever needed before. I looked into my mother's sad blue eyes, squeezed the gloves and ball even harder and waited ...

The words came hard and my mother's voice cracked as they passed her lips, "Your Father is dying, he has a disease called Huntington's."

I felt weak and the baseball fell from my hand. I watched the ball bounce and then roll across the kitchen floor as tears began to run down my face. No words came from my dry throat as I watched the baseball come to rest against the stove. I stared at it for a moment, which seemed an eternity. As I stared, a hand came down and picked up the ball. I looked up and saw my father. He smiled, and I tried but could not return it. All I had for him were tears!

    I am older and maybe a little wiser since that day. I am happily married with a loving wife and a beautiful daughter now six years old, who I am sure would protest and insist she is six and a half. I look back on that time not with sadness but remembering my father's smiling face. I was taught a bittersweet lesson in that moment so many years ago – one that has burned a small hole in my soul. I learned the importance of embracing and enjoying life. Cherishing every moment, every smile and every tear is a way of healing even a gaping wound.
    My daughter and I play catch every chance we get just to see the joy on each other's face. Two well-used baseball gloves and a ball will always sit on the chair in the hall waiting for the next game.

Jeffrey S Oxford Ottawa ON

He Loves Me Anyway

We were standing side by side at church on Sunday morning. I can't remember much about the Mass except that the church was crowded and we were somewhere near the back. As my father and I stood resting our hands on the pew in front, my dad reached out his little finger and hooked it over mine. Fear clenched the pit of my stomach! I moved away, stunned at my own reaction. What was I afraid of?

My dad and I were kindred souls in many ways and understood each other from the inside. I marveled at the number of times, throughout my growing up years, that we knew what the other was thinking before it was voiced. When I considered the possibility of reincarnation, I wondered if our rapport could be due to an accumulation of lifetimes together.

At this point in our lives, I was living with my husband and children a long distance from my parents' home so we visited only once a year or so. My father was an alcoholic who had begun drinking about ten years before we found ourselves together on this summer morning. Times had been very difficult – my mother's suffering as the wife of an alcoholic was severe and ongoing. Although my dad was never physically abusive, the change in his personality and his inability to function normally while intoxicated had seriously strained their marriage relationship.

It was impossible to make family plans which included my father, because his pattern was to drink until he passed out. Before he went into long periods of alcohol-induced sleep, he would assail family members with the same question asked over and over until they became angry with him. The nature of the question seemed immaterial as was the number of times it was answered – usually calmly at first then with increasing irritation and even rage as the answer only produced a loud, obnoxious repetition of the question. It was as if my father believed he was loathsome and would not rest until he proved to himself that we did, in fact, hate him.

When he reached out for my confidence and love that Sunday morning, despite my sorrow for his affliction, I panicked and shut myself off from him. Maybe I believed that closeness to dad undermined my support for my mother and the long night I had just spent empathizing with her anguish. Still, how could improving my relationship with dad be anything but helpful?? Was it safer for me not to be privy to his pain and isolation? In the aftermath of that moment, I was ashamed, guilty, diminished.

Some years later, beating the odds, my father recovered from his addiction, wiser and stronger than he had ever been, with a new vision of the world. For me, the ultimate outcome of this moment of fear came when I recognized the power of forgiveness. My father held no bitterness toward me – my error evaporated in the fullness of his love.

Judi Cumming   Vancouver BC

Mariah of Milwaukee

She was simply standing there,
holding on for dear life to a light pole at the intersection.
I did not notice her as I approached the corner,
hurrying and laughing with a friend, late for a meeting.

Her gaze and her words singled me out,
"Can you wait with me for a while?"
My explanation limped,
"We're on our way back to a meeting."

"You could wait with me, if you wanted to."
"No, I really cannot. We need to get back to that hotel over there."
Her eyes pleaded,
and my heart struggled to respond.

The street was wide and
traffic sped by as people returned to work.
The wind blew hard and harsh:
she was afraid to cross the street.

"Let's walk across together," I suggested,
taking her arm as we set out into the street. She drew
back – unused to being touched by another,
"No, no, you are pulling me!"

Calming her, I tried again;
I think she took my elbow.
Once on the other side of the street,
she scuttled away, disappearing as fast as she appeared.

I carried her with me for a long time after this encounter,
aware of my own fears of strong winds and strangers.
I felt ashamed that I had acted as '*a person of consequence*',

too busy to spend a little time with someone in need.
I did not get her name and
were we to meet again, I would not recognize her.
In my mind she is Mariah,
a simple soul, daring me to pause a little in a busy day.

Mariah *(Greek for wisdom)*, like the wind,
a breath of God, moving wherever she would,
opening, challenging and inviting me
to *wait with her for just a little while.*

Mary Elizabeth Looby, GNSH
Fallsington PA

Running on Empty

Some years ago, I was employed by a financial institution as a senior loan officer. It was a job I truly loved. I loved it because for the most part, I was helping people. Helping some to obtain mortgages for their first home, helping some out of financial difficulties and helping others to make their dreams come true. But as time went by the job became more and more demanding and eventually, I began to experience burnout. There never seemed to be enough hours to complete the work waiting to be done. It was all I could do at the end of the day to go home and crawl into bed, exhausted. All chores and even important personal matters were mostly neglected.

One day while driving home from work, I heard a voice speak to me as if it came from someone sitting next to me in the car. But, there was nobody in the car; I was alone. I heard this voice clearly say to me, "Go immediately and get your engine oil checked!"

I was startled at first, then knew instinctively that this was the voice of an inner guidance. A wonderful calmness came over me--penetrating me completely, mentally and physically. Anxiety, fatigue, exhaustion were gone as this sense of peace permeated me and seemed to extend outward around me.

I stopped at a service station about two blocks away. After checking the oil, the attendant turned to me and said with some concern: "Lady, if you had driven another half mile your engine would have seized on you. You have no oil in the engine!"

Once the oil was replenished, I returned home. The glorious calmness was still with me and I knew for certain that I was spiritually guided and protected at all times.

Since then, I am more ready to receive the intuitive messages I believe come to us all the time. Listening to them assures me that I am filled with God's love and all I need do is extend it, whenever, wherever and however I can.

Judy Miller   Abbotsford BC

Finding my Voice

It is early May 2001. A cold wind blowing off Lake Ontario penetrates deeply causing a chill to settle in my bones. I find myself sitting 20 yards from the water's edge, surrounded by a core of women all drawn to the same spot, for the same reason. We have gathered to celebrate the life and passing of our cherished friend and sister, Claudi. To know Claudi, was to know strength, love, laughter, gentleness and a zest for life - for she represented all of those qualities and more.

It is strange; tears are few, but ripples of laughter are streaming out across the shimmering lake. Claudi's last wish is to have her ashes scattered over the waters of Lake Ontario, for in her lifetime, she had often found comfort and solace in its ever-changing surface and shores.

A womyn's drumming circle has formed. Womyn is an inclusive group of women of all ethnicities and orientations who use drumming to bring healing to our fractured world. A steady, powerful rhythm is keeping time to the beat of waves as they roll in and break up on the jagged rocks lining the shore, connecting all of us gathered here in its Taoist cadence.

I peer around; the sun is reflecting off the water, making it difficult to see. The beating of the drums fills my senses. It is almost surreal. My thoughts go to Claudi...and her battle with breast cancer, a journey that we happen to share. I am drawn back to her final words to me just a few short months before: "You don't have to do this journey alone...reach out...break your silence."

Suddenly, the drums go silent. The women who have gathered are invited up to say a few words in memory of a precious friend. Now, the tears begin to flow. More laughter also resounds across the rolling meadow where we have come to say our final good-byes.

I am cold from the inside out. The relentless icy wind belies the bright sunshine. My weight loss since starting chemotherapy has made it difficult for me to generate enough body heat to stay warm. As I listen to story after story, I find myself staring past the memorial altar that we have built for Claudi, out onto the water.

A woman is standing at the water's edge. She is dressed in a black leather jacket and black jeans. Her cropped short grey hair is just touching the top of her collar. Slowly, she turns to face me. I can't make out her face because of the glare from the sun as it reflects off the water. Then, the woman begins to move toward me. She is smiling. Her stride is strong and deliberate. As she gets closer, my heart skips a beat...my breathing stops. It is Claudi. I shake my head, blink my eyes to try and re-focus. She is still there. I can't speak. I can't move. She speaks to me...."Now is the time to break your silence...I am here...you are strong and you know what to do and say". And then, in less than a moment she is gone.

Was what just happened real? I begin to feel a warm sensation fill my body. My cold, tense muscles begin to loosen. I find myself rising out of my chair and moving slowly toward the stage where the microphone is placed. I sense I will find the words once I begin to speak.

On that early May morning, I found my strength, my voice and my courage to break the silence and speak about my own journey with breast cancer. And, as with Claudi, the womyn's community has since embraced me and I am not alone.

Thank you, Claudi for that gentle prod.

Nita Michelle Coderre
(aka Sarah Emery)　　　Kingston ON

Sufficient Grace

I have always loved and been fascinated by the history of my congregation. The Religious Hospitallers of St. Joseph, the modern name of our Roman Catholic order of nursing Sisters, was founded in 1636 by Jerome LeRoyer of France. Jerome was not a Church leader – far from it. He was a young tax collector with a family.

Imagine his confusion when, in February 1630, he received an overwhelming three-fold mandate from God. He was inspired to found a religious order of women to care for the sick and most needy, to colonize the island of Montreal half a world away and to send members of the order to look after the sick there! After three years of hesitation, he acted on his inspiration and began to do what was necessary to accomplish these goals. Miraculously, he managed, despite unbelievable odds, to achieve all of them.

First, he organized the small group of original hospitallers to care for the sick in LaFleche, France. Then, in 1642, Sieur de Maisonneuve and Jeanne Mance arrived in the New World to establish the city of Ville Marie on the island of Montreal and set up a Hotel Dieu Hospital there. Maisonneuve and Mance are much more famous than the man who recruited them – the persevering LeRoyer, the force behind the expedition. Only the third task remained.

In 1659, three Sisters, known then as Daughters of St. Joseph, arrived at Ville Marie after a long, hazardous ocean voyage: Judith Moreau, Catherine Mace and Marie Maillet. As I read about them, I marvelled at how they survived even the first winter, let alone the many decades of harsh pioneer life that awaited them.

One January day in 1999, I was absorbed in the details of their circumstances, when a blast of icy winter wind rattled the windows of my convent room, sweeping my mind back in time. I was there with my sisters, thousands of miles from home, without money or even sanction from the Church, accepting with faith the challenge to care for the sick and wounded in an unknown land.

Winter Reverie

Today winter has come with a bang
Fine driven snow blown by gusty winds
Into knee-high drifts.
I hesitate to walk even the short street
between our house and the hospital.
Instead, in the cosy warmth of my room
I let my mind wander
Down three hundred years and more.

What a shock it must have been
That first winter in Ville Marie
When our three Mothers came.
All of them gentlewomen
From well-to-do homes in temperate France
How did they survive the bitter cold
The lack of proper food
The fear of Iroquois raids
The fatigue of daily caring for the sick?

God said to Jerome, and to them, and to us
"My grace is sufficient for thee."
And so today I pray
"Dear Judith, and Catherine and Marie,
From your high place in heaven
Look down on us your sisters of another century
Obtain for us the grace we need
For the winter storms of our lives."

Sister Mary Coderre, RHSJ
Amherstview ON

CONNECTION

My Father who art in Heaven

A message on my voicemail at work summoned me to the hospital; the message said my father was dying. My father, although almost 80 years old, had not been sick, so this was quite a shock.

I rushed to get there, in time to ... say goodbye, offer support to my mother, and, I am not sure what else. I arrived to find my mother and two of my sisters in the room with my father - who looked fine, although he had a vacant stare on his face. He was not responding to our questions and didn't even seem to be aware we were in the room. One of my sisters shrugged her shoulders when I gave her a questioning look that said, 'He doesn't look like he's dying'. Later she told me that he had not had a heart attack as they first thought, but was suffering from a severe swelling of the brain.

Because my mother and sisters had been there since the previous night, I offered to stay with Dad while they went home and got some much-needed sleep. Sitting with my father as he faded from this mortal life, I came to know the depth of his faith. We had been told that most of his brain's functioning was gone and that it was only a matter of time before he died.

In the quiet of the night I found myself praying, 'Hail Mary, full of grace, the Lord is with thee ...' in my mind. This was not entirely foreign to me, since we had often recited the rosary as a family when I was a child, but still, it was a little surprising as I had not done so recently.

I don't remember starting the prayer, or for how long I had been praying. I looked up at my father and noticed his lips were moving. I continued to pray silently as I walked over to his bed and leaned in to listen to his almost inaudible whisper: "Blessed art thou amongst women; and blessed is the fruit of thy womb, Jesus."

We were praying in unison! I couldn't believe it – being able to comprehend 'prayer' in his apparent mental condition should have been impossible; and yet, this is exactly what I would have expected from a man whose faith was as strong and deep as my dad's. The undeniable fact that somehow we were connected through this prayer was, and is, very comforting to me.

About fifteen minutes later, as my father's last moments of consciousness approached, he amazed me again as, for the last time, he expressed his love for my mother. I told him Mom would be there soon and he clearly said 'Love'. How fitting that his last words and thoughts would be to express his love for God and for his wife of almost 60 years.

My father's example, both during his life and at his death, was a powerful and moving display of faith. Since his death, I have sought to renew my relationship with a loving God. Concepts and beliefs I had been taught as a child, and followed blindly, are being looked at through adult eyes.

I only hope that when my time on this earth draws to a close, that my relationship with God and with my wife will be as strong and deeply rooted as was my father's.

Dave Coderre	Ottawa ON

Katie's Gift

I had started my career teaching high school in the regular program, and had later changed to French Immersion and moved down to the intermediate grades (ten to twelve-year-olds), but had never thought of the primary level. When I was asked to take a grade two, I thought I could handle it as seven-year-olds could at least sit still for more than five minutes.

But when the next request was for me to teach a Junior Kindergarten, I was completely out of my realm. There were little creatures heading in every direction, bodies clinging to my legs, wooden trucks running into my ankles, children crying to go home, shoes needing to be tied and noses to be wiped, glue and paint adorning my clothes, and sand, snow or mud on my feet depending on the outdoor play season. However, I tried my best, and by February had succeeded in getting the room full of four-year-olds to sit in a circle for up to ten minutes!

'I'll make it to June and then switch grades', was my thought for the day, every day.

One day in May I was told that Katie, one of my students, would be leaving as her family was moving to California. On her last day, her parents came in and watched proudly as she participated in my class, demonstrating her new French vocabulary. With blue eyes sparkling and blond ponytails bouncing, Katie pranced about the circle, paper butterfly in hand, landing correctly on the flower of the chosen color, while we sang "Papillon, papillon vole a rouge , jaune, etc."

When it came time for her to leave, she came over to give me a hug. As Katie's chubby little arms went around my neck, she whispered "Bye Madame" and my eyes filled with tears (not a common thing for me). I suddenly realized that I would really miss her.

In spite of myself, I had become closely attached to her and all the little trusting souls in my class.

In that moment I knew that this was where I wanted to be. I continued teaching kindergarten for 17 more years until my recent retirement.

Kathy Bissett   Ottawa ON

Guardians of Land and Sea

In 1992 I had a show at the Harrison Art Gallery in British Columbia. The native people of the area related deeply to my work: extended nature photographs with titles including Guardians of Land and Sea, Sha(wo)man, Habitat of a Lost Tribe, After the Potlatch. Some of the Indians brought flowers from their gardens, relating the colours to my work, and placed rocks in the corners of the room. A sha(wo)man went from work to work, blessing each one with cedar water while chanting softly. My husband Frank did not give it much significance, but I remarked, "We can never be blessed enough."

When the show was over, Frank loaded our camper with the 40 photo-paintings, and drove home. He parked the truck in our carport but failed to secure the parking brake. I glanced out our kitchen window and screamed: "The truck is moving!"

Frank could not run out fast enough to stop it. Our vehicle moved in an arc, as if guided by an invisible hand, and ran onto the curb where it left a deep indent. It had just missed our neighbour's carport, and had avoided the hill - a road to certain disaster. It stopped at the only 'safe' place on its journey, evading a wooden post, shrubs, fence, dogs, cats and playing children!

Remembering my show, I see in a blur the opening ceremony, some sales, the chatter with visitors, the musical entertainment. But the deepest resonance in my soul comes from the memory of the spiritual involvement of the Indian visitors whose blessings - I believe - protected my work and prevented a catastrophe.

In recent years, my work as a volunteer for the Hospice Society has given me opportunities to fully understand how powerful blessings can be. To say to a dying person, 'God bless you', is something new in my vocabulary, but I have found it to be a wonderful gift of comfort to any patient who is a believer. When in the last slice of my patient's life talking has ceased, I may sing softly into his ear, hoping that the song's soft vibration will ease the dying person's pain and transport him gently to the 'Beautiful Isles of Somewhere'.

The kind 'Guardians of Land and Sea' have entered my spirit. I have found my own way to pass on their blessings.

Margot Wawra   Abbotsford BC

A Father's Gift

My Dad was dying and I do not mean slowly or inevitably. This was something that would happen very soon, within days. He was not old, just 68. Before falling ill, he had been a large, robust man, made that way by the hard physical work of his youth. He had lung cancer and had known for a period of time that he was past any hope of cure or even significant arrest of the inexorable progress of the disease. By the time of this moment, he had become calm and accepting of the inevitable.

I was living at the opposite end of the country from him. When that country is Canada, that is a long way. I lived in Nova Scotia with our young and growing family. Dad was in BC, his lifelong home. Over the course of his advancing disease, we managed to make several visits and I had a number of important and personal talks with him. But, this is only background to what I want to share and the powerful last lesson he taught me.

My brother called me to say the end was very near and if I was going to see Dad one last time, I had better get on a plane for Vancouver. As much as I wanted to do so, there was a pilots' strike and air travel in Canada was snarled like rush-hour traffic in downtown Toronto. I leapt through innumerable hoops and called upon many kindly people to get a flight booked from Halifax to Vancouver. In fact, my trip took me from Halifax to Montreal, Philadelphia, Chicago and Seattle, with the last leg by car to Vancouver, after waiting too long for the next standby seat out of Seattle.

I got to my Dad's bedside a day sooner than any of us thought possible according to my original travel plan. He was lucid enough to know I was there and to be agitated at thinking he had lost a day. He knew my travel plan and thought it should be Monday if I were there. He thought he had lost

Sunday in a haze of morphine and other pain-killers. He had not, and I add this only to show that he was fully there when last I saw him. We talked a little - not much. In truth, there was not much left to say, at least not in spoken words. It was late in the evening, maybe 11 p.m. or so. Dad had drifted off to sleep, holding my hand lightly. That in itself was amazing enough. He was not a man who normally showed emotion nor was in any way 'touchy feely'.

His doctor wanted to speak with my brother and me, so we left the room to hear what he had to say. Mostly, it was kind of a gentle 'pep talk' to help us cope. In truth, I don't really remember much of what he said. If Dad had reached his own private place in the dying process, I guess I had too.

The nurses had been wonderful and one of the ladies told us that Dad would sleep through the night now, so there was not much for us to do there. She told us to get some sleep as well. It seemed to be good advice and we prepared to leave for the night.

I had left my coat in Dad's room. I went back to get it. As I entered his room and looked at this obscenely diminished and fragile form under the hospital sheets a thought, no, a 'knowing' flowed over me. Our Dad was leaving, had maybe already gone. He had waited for me and now it was finished. I knew this as an absolute certainty deep within my heart and it was OK. I was calm. There was nothing I could do to change things and I knew then as I know now, his last gift was letting me understand and accept. I whispered, "Goodnight, Dad." But, in my heart I knew I meant goodbye. I knew that whether I actually saw him again or not, our journey together was over. He was now free of everything holding him back.

Two hours later the hospital called to say he had died quietly without waking again.

Dan Cumming   Vancouver BC

Threads of Ancestry

I was five when my grandpa sat me on his knee. "Did you know Stephen, you're the eldest son of the eldest son of the eldest son?" Once I got that, after many questions, I bloomed with pride. I'm somewhere on the line. I'm important, like a prince in a big long history. Even after the self-importance melted away in adolescence, I was left with the certainty that I was, at least, never alone.

Through times of barely making rent...Standing in the EI line ...Airline turbulence to Narita... Facing down a 6'5" student gang leader in an inner city school basement... Being dismissed by money grubbing bosses trying to blame me for not getting seats-in-desks to fill private school quotas ...Watching dear friends get around in golf carts bundled up in disability donations...Through the benefits and memorials...'I know I'm one' as Pete Townsend sings.

No matter what - to a large, extended group somewhere out there, I am unique - the eldest of the eldest of the eldest. Always will be. Grandpa told me once.

Nobody can unstitch the threads of ancestry. No one can shift the order of birth, no matter how early the death may come. No matter what happens. No matter, whatever. We are all someone to someone. And I am the eldest of the eldest of the eldest.

And of that I can be proud.

Stephen Emery   Vancouver BC

Burnt Offerings

My mother recently passed away. She had been experiencing a series of health setbacks over the last months of her life. However, when the end came, it happened suddenly and peacefully. My mother had talked to me about her life extensively over the last months. It was obvious to me that she was putting her house in order. I had worked with palliative patients in hospice who had behaved quite similarly. I tried to prepare myself and my sister for the inevitable. But my sister, who had shared a home with my mother for the last fifteen years, was completely devastated.

As I had undergone surgery a few days before my mother's death, I was unable to be with my sister to go through funeral arrangements. I was heartsick about it. My surgery had been urgent and arranged quickly. Its timing meant that a long-planned visit home was cancelled. (My husband had a work conference and I had made arrangements to travel with him.) I would still have arrived four days too late to see my mother, but I would have been there to help my sister through the funeral and those first few days. Instead a cremation was planned, then a burial of the urn at my father's gravesite that I could attend at a later date.

On the day of my mom's cremation, I came to the realization that the day was my late father's birthday. She had missed him greatly. Grief overwhelmed me. I was inconsolable, crying at everything. To distract myself, I decided to make soup for my husband who would be returning later in the day from his business trip. I had not yet cooked since coming home from hospital.

My mom had prided herself on her culinary ability. She also loved to laugh and was always ready with a joke or a funny story. One of her favorites was about a man who had remarried after his first wife died. He was very happy in his new marriage with his second wife but made no bones about the fact that she was not the cook his first wife had been. One day the new wife was idling time away talking to her neighbor and lost track of the hour. She glanced up and saw her husband entering the road to the house. Yelling her goodbyes, she ran into the kitchen to find that she had burned dinner. It was too late to do anything except carefully scrape off as much of the burn as she could. Nervously she served him his meal. He ate with gusto and beamed at his new wife as he exclaimed: "For once, you have made a meal as good as my first wife!"

Yes, I burned the soup! In over 30 years of cooking, I can't recall the last time I burned anything. I started crying again. Then my mother's story came to my mind. My mother was giving me a message she knew I would understand. I had to laugh. She had played out her favorite story on me. She was letting me know it was all right that things hadn't worked out as I had planned. My not being there when she died was okay, just like the wife whose 'mistake' discovered the secret of a 'good meal'. Nothing in life is perfect. Although I wasn't there to say goodbye, my mother gave me her farewell in a manner I'll never forget – burnt offerings for my husband!

Marika Kohut   Victoria BC

Nine to One

He asks me if I, too, believe that he is dying. I tell him that it only matters what he believes. That, in the end, what he truly believes in his heart will happen.

But alas, yes that's the whole key ...knowing what you really believe. You know what you want to happen...you know what you wish would happen...you know what you pray will happen.

He tells me he doesn't pray. He never has. He believes in people. He believes in the goodness of people. He resents talk of hell. Nor does he believe in heaven. He believes death is like a non-stop sleep. I wonder if he's considered the possibility of a non-stop dream in that sleep?

He tells me that he believes the universe owes him more. He tells me he believes he deserves more. He's always been a good person. Helped out anyone and everyone he could...has never once said no to someone in need. He has been an exceptional family man, husband, father.

His wife says he always made her feel like a princess. He grins and says that's because she always made him feel like a king. It nearly breaks my heart. Yes, he deserves more than this. He deserves better. That's what he believes. I ask him if he believes that a person always gets what he deserves. He quietly replies, "No."

I lead him through a meditation. We talk about not hating the cancer and looking at it like an enemy, but instead embracing the knowledge that comes with this cancer. We talk about surrounding it and ourselves in a wonderful golden healing light, like the sun shining down on a warm day...let the light overtake the darkness that is inside. Let the light shine on the cancer...what could it be?

He had a father who was unkind - very unkind - to him and to his mother. He's too small to help her. She gets hurt often. We surround this father in the same light until it is so bright that he disappears in its radiance.

Silently now we sit together. He says simply, "I was afraid". I know he means of his father and his father's actions. Has he forgiven?

His shoulders lower slightly, he begins to yawn, one big yawn after another. I look around as I begin to yawn...the whole room is yawning...patients and visitors and a young nurse...There are nine of us ...synchronized! Through the yawn, we begin to laugh at each other's gaping mouths.

Just at that moment, the sun shines a warm, golden light into the room. We are caught in laughter and then in tears and yes, wonder. Here we all are ... laughing and crying, sad yet joyous, connected - that's it, without a doubt...nine of us marveling together in gratitude for that.

Cynthia Lee-Strawford   Peachland BC

Blowing in the Wind

Hong Kong is like no place on earth. It zings and bustles with a vitality that literally vibrates your core as the crowds swallow you up. Everyone rushes with single purpose and people tend to mind their own business no matter what crosses their paths.

I had the privilege of living and working in Hong Kong for four years from 1995 to 1998 and commuting daily between the New Territories and old Wanchai. My commute to the office was an experience in Hong Kong logistics. Just imagine at least three million people in motion during morning and evening rush hours to and from work or school within 200 square kilometers - compared to Toronto, Canada, which has three times the area and half the number of commuters.

We lived in the New Territories and my morning began with a short trip on a light bus (a sixteen-seater vehicle), which I boarded at the entrance to my apartment building. This bus, driven by one of the many zealous 'I can complete this route in just under the speed of sound' drivers, delivered me to the train station where I caught the first available train into which I could squeeze. Depending on the timing, I might have to wait for two or three trains before I could continue my journey.

Once aboard, I enjoyed close up and personal contact with many polite strangers. My train took me to the mouth of the tunnel from Kowloon to Hong Kong Island. There I caught a double decker bus, once again packed with people - thankfully most everyone showered daily! Through the exhaust filled tunnel we would lurch, up-gear, down-gear, until we finally reached daylight at the other end. Two stops above ground, which is the time it took me to work the crowd to get to the exit door, and I was released to walk two more blocks to the office. Reverse this scenario for the trip home.

I was in the habit of carrying my camera to capture street scenes. One day on my two-block trek from my final bus stop to the office, I saw a pigeon sitting under a parked double decker bus. The picture was a winner – fat pigeon sitting motionless in front of the rear wheel - dwarfed by the sheer magnitude of this massive bus. Picture taken, I was putting my camera away when I heard the roar of exhaust as the driver put the bus in gear. I knew immediately what was going to happen, and helplessly watched as the bus started moving and the pigeon did not. In a slow motion heartbeat, the poor little bird was flipped under the wheel and all that remained was a bulge of blowing feathers on the road.

I could only stand there staring, shaken by the quick and sudden death. Slowly I realized that many others were also standing quietly, gazing at this luckless pigeon, and immediately I felt a shared bond of vulnerability.

Then, as if heeding some silent signal, everyone suddenly dispersed and the sidewalk was bustling with activity once more. The moment was over, but that short, powerful interaction with a group of total strangers has remained with me, reminding me that at some level, we are not really strangers at all.

Allison Stokholm   Barrie ON

FREEDOM

The Last Taboo

As we lay naked side by side in bed, the predawn glow barely dispelling the darkness, I smiled at his sleeping form. With him, I had done the unspeakable: violated my ultimate taboo. Me, middle-aged, a virgin when I'd married 25 years ago and until now, happily faithful to my husband.

Philippe would be returning to France in a matter of hours and I would never see him again. He was a man wrestling with inner fears, burdened by guilt and determined to experience life via sex. When I first met him two weeks earlier at the start of the course we were taking, I quickly wrote him off as a desperate, unattractive womanizer. His age (mid-60's) qualified him as a 'dirty old man' in my books. However, as I got to know him better, listened to the questions he asked in class, watched him interact with others in the group, my opinion was transformed. I began to see him as bright, beautiful, sensitive, funny, vulnerable, extremely sexy and definitely scary. He threatened my long-established, inflexible rule: no matter what excuses were made to justify it, extramarital sex was wrong. This idea had remained firm in my mind, despite the fact that I imagined myself to be non-judgmental and well past considering issues as 'black or white'.

Through the years of my marriage I had occasionally met men I found interesting and sexually attractive, but never before had I seriously considered 'cheating' on my husband. Now here I was, after a night of intimate, passionate sex with an almost stranger, still amazed that I felt so peaceful. It was as if, in that moment, a light had turned on in my closet of 'absolutes' revealing it to be empty! My last 'absolute' was gone. Before that, I might have pretended to accept a friend's transgression in this area, but would have still considered it just that. Now, I was one of 'those' women – 'an adulteress who had shamed herself and made a cuckold of her husband'! I found myself dredging up all the vile words I could think of to describe myself – whore, harlot, slut - none of them seemed to stick.

Nevertheless, when I told my husband about it, fear was trembling in my voice. I felt compelled to tell him but was not sure he'd understand. He was quiet a moment before he said, "I love you and I trust your judgment." He went on to tell me how proud he was of me for making a decision that he knew I would find extremely difficult and for opening myself to an experience that was clearly so important to me. Sometimes, the ripple effect is as glorious as the moment itself.

Years afterward, I feel no remorse but rather a certain exhilaration that I had dared challenge beliefs taught to me from childhood that I had held, unexamined, for so long.

Anonymous

Round Trip?

Sydney, Australia. February 16, 1999. That's the day I stopped being afraid and realized who the real coward was. His name was Adam. He was a backpacking through Europe adventure gone terribly wrong. He was in my life for almost three years: part of it in Europe, some of it in a one-bedroom apartment in Canada, and thirty-one very long days in Australia.

For the first two and half years I thought if I could change a bit, or be really understanding, he'd go back to being as nice as he was in the first week of the relationship. No such luck. He never hit me. He only twisted my wrist behind my back a couple of times, and made sure to give me an everyday reminder that I was lucky he loved me, because no one else would want me. He did things like that, among others that I won't go into, to scare me into staying with him. Strangely enough, it worked... for a while.

January 17th, 1999. I was on a plane to Sydney. The plan was to move there for a year; we'd get engaged and then move back to Canada. I changed the plan. On my second day there I held my breath and told him we were finished. That did not go well. He threw up. And then got very angry, and then very sad, and then very angry again. Why I didn't get back on a plane that minute and come home I don't know. I guess I was still scared of what he might say, or more importantly, do. Every morning I would go for a run and spend most of the time praying for God to give me the strength and courage to walk away from this person.

February 15th. The praying started to work. I put a quarter in my shoe, went for a run, and called the airline from a phone booth. I booked a ticket home for two days later, the 17th. Now the only thing left to do was to tell him I was finally leaving and never coming back. I was terrified.

    February 16th. We were driving home from a night out with Adam's friends. I told him I was leaving. In hindsight I probably shouldn't have done that while he was driving a fast-moving vehicle, but hey, at least I did it. He freaked out - yelling obscenities, driving like a crazy person. This kind of outburst from him usually made me cry. Not this time. I just stared at him. It was as though something in my brain finally clicked into a new gear. I laughed over his screaming and said calmly, "You are ridiculous." I suddenly realized that I had absolutely nothing to fear from this person. He was, and always had been, more scared than me.

    February 17th. I boarded a 747 bound for Toronto - no longer afraid.

Danielle Krysa   Toronto ON

Border Run

I'd been travelling Myanmar for twenty-six days on a twenty-eight day visa.

I'd made my way to Kayin State in the south, where I was about to unfold a master plan I had been dreaming about for weeks. I was sweating with anticipation.

Myanmar (formerly known as Burma) is bordered by Thailand, Laos, China, India, and Bangladesh, and foreign travellers are forbidden to cross any of these borders by land – in or out of the country. To get to Myanmar you must fly into Mandalay or Yangon, where close tabs can be kept on foreigners. These restrictions have been enforced by a ruthless military dictatorship for almost half a century.

The military has labeled many areas of the country 'black', where foreigners are not allowed to enter. In some of these areas the military is hiding the forced labour of men, women, and children, who have been taken from their villages and made to work on roads. In other 'black' areas there is violent fighting with minority groups who are trying desperately to defend their rights.

The Karen inhabiting most of Kayin State are one such group. Vastly out-powered and outnumbered, the Karen resort to bloody guerrilla warfare tactics, often ambushing vehicles along the remote jungle roads. Kayin State is thus very 'black' and no foreigner is permitted east of the capital Hpa-an.

I had traveled to Hpa-an, and my 'master plan' was to continue east to the border with Thailand. The dirt road crossed a steep range of mountains covered in heavy jungle, and was impassable every rainy season. In the dry season, one small, aluminum-paneled diesel bus struggled through 140 kilometers of mountains to the Thai border every second day – a twelve-hour journey.

This bus was an easy target for an attack. But barring an ambush, all I had to do was bribe my way through six military checkpoints stationed along the way. Lowly government soldiers make eight to ten US dollars a month, and I had already learned their willingness to cooperate for a small 'present'. Myanmar is a country rampant with corruption, and a five-dollar US note is your ticket to *anywhere*.

Across the border into Thailand was Mae Sot, my destination. Mae Sot was a dusty little town where some old friends of mine were living. Part of my dream was the triumphant march across the border and boasting to them about what I had just done.

No one in Myanmar said my plan was going to work. I'd met foreigners and locals alike who had warned me against travelling deep into 'black' territory.

"They shoot up buses all the time!" an over-anxious backpacker had exclaimed. True, a bus had been ambushed last year in a bloody Karen offensive, but it didn't happen *all the time*, I thought.

"They won't let you on the bus..." a young local told me, "not if they have any sense." True, the driver could get thrown in jail for letting a foreigner on the bus, but *only if he got caught*, I thought.

"Even if you get on the bus, the first checkpoint will stop you," preached a guesthouse owner whom I had hoped would be keen on my master plan. And true, they probably would, unless I offered them *a reason not to*, I thought. Nothing fazed me; I was drunk on a potent mix of stubbornness and madness.

The morning of my twenty-seventh day in Myanmar arrived. I'd been tossing and turning all night, buzzing with anxiety and anticipation over the imminent day of attack. Armed with a pocketful of 'fivers', a carton of cigarettes and two bottles of Mandalay rum, I hit the street at 4:30 a.m. for the 5:00 a.m. bus. "I need to go to the border, I have to get to Thailand!" I told the driver.

He let me on the bus.

I chose a seat in the middle of the empty bus, pressed my face against the glass and peered outside. The stray dogs I had passed on the road lay motionless in the dust. An old man lingered in the pre-dawn darkness. Plastic chairs made the only sound as a teashop owner set up for the morning rush. Minutes went by - the driver sat still in his worn leather chair. I thought about all the time I had invested conceiving this plan, convincing myself it would work, and preparing for the difficulties ahead.

Suddenly something changed. *Who am I kidding?* I thought to myself. *There is nothing I need to prove.*

All the built up tension dissolved. My body relaxed. My breathing was slow. My spirits were high. Reality clicked sharply into focus - I had one day left on my visa to get back to Yangon and fly out of Myanmar.

I stepped off the bus.

Neil Chantler	Vancouver BC

Choices

I went for a walk in Beacon Hill Park in Victoria, B.C. Ordinarily when I go for a walk I'm trying to get a workout so I put on a walkman and go fast. I was doing just that on this particular day. But then, contrary to my usual routine, I decided to stop and sit on a bench beside one of the ponds in the park.

It was a beautiful, sunny day. I was surrounded by majestic trees and an inviting little lake. As I sat there, I began to understand the importance of occasionally slowing down my pace and taking in the beauty around me.

I had just started the bar exam course – a demanding ten-week program that is required in order to practice law in British Columbia - and was feeling stressed about this new challenge.

As I sat on the bench, a very intense feeling seemed to 'come over me' - I became aware that my attitude determines how challenges in my life will work out. During the ten or fifteen minutes I sat there, I felt extremely empowered and physically energized.

I had a strong sense that I had the choice as to how I would view the hurdles in my life: difficult or challenging situations could only upset me if I let them. I came to an understanding about how to deal with stressful situations. I realized that I have the ability and inner strength to guide myself through them and that I must trust myself to do exactly that.

As I went through the bar course these realizations were definitely tested and tried at times, but I still try to be guided by this approach. My 'revelation in the park' ultimately influences the way I try to deal with life in general and especially with stressful situations that scare me.

Janna Cumming Vancouver BC

Of Death and Thanksgiving

I attended both my parents through their dying. It was cherished, life-altering experience for me to be invited to be present, for which I will always be grateful. They both died in their seventies of cancer, at home, on Thanksgiving weekend, two years apart. Despite the medical cause of death, I think both of them had their own reasons for deciding it was time.

My mother left first, providing a template for my dad to use later. As the end grew closer for him, it became clear he had paid close attention, while caring for her so tenderly, and learned from her example how to make the transition with grace.

One of the hardest aspects for me to witness was the continuum of physical degeneration. Vibrant and attractive, even into their senior years, they grew pale, thin, tired - loose mottled skin over brittle bones, gasping short, raspy breaths. And yet, it is hard to explain that in the midst of the painful and grotesque, there was a prevailing, pure beauty, which seemed to reassure me that, at a level beyond my ability to fully understand, everything was in order.

Finally, in a long, silent instant, the breathing stopped: astoundingly, so did the beauty – leaving behind only an ugly, shrunken mass on the bed. Twice it happened; twice my reaction was the same. I felt no attachment to it! I stared blankly at the cast off shell and saw only a worn out instrument discarded because it was no longer useful. I was overwhelmed by the certainty that without it they were infinitely better off – free to be however they wished, unconstrained by form.

Now I sometimes sense them around me - one or both; a wise, powerful presence far beyond the parents I knew before. They come to comfort, inspire, light my way – to help as much as I will let them.

Judi Cumming   Vancouver BC

Peace and Joy

Some years ago I attended a fundraising event for the Tibetan monks in exile. At the start of the event the audience was asked to refrain from clapping as what we were there to share was the monks daily devotional practice and not a 'concert'. The people in the audience all looked around nervously not knowing how to respond. The facilitator explained the sequence of events and again reminded us that we were in fact observing the monks in their prayers.

The monks started playing their long flutes, gongs and bells. Their voices, made clear by many years of chanting, vibrated as one with the sounds of their instruments. They danced out many of their prayers also - exuberant bouncing steps with their instruments in hand, never missing a note. Occasionally a monk would burst into a somersault, startling us. It did not take long for a remarkable feeling of peace to descend upon the auditorium. When the monks finally concluded their prayers, there was not a movement in the audience. It was as if we had all been transfixed. We left mostly in a silence that felt sacred.

At that time, I had been going through turmoil in my personal life. I was having difficulties resolving changes that had occurred. My mental anguish was great. It had left me sleepless many nights as I reviewed matters in my mind trying to come to terms with them. But that night I fell into a sounder, more peaceful sleep than I had in many months.

Suddenly, at some time in the night, I sat bolt upright, fully awake and aware. Directly above me in a cone of light was one of the monks. He was laughing and so happy with his hands in a prayer position over his heart. He laughed and laughed. Instantly I knew what I had been denying myself was to feel joy. The monk was showing me how to get through my turmoil. Laugh. Stop taking everything so seriously. Life is full of joy. Take the time to be at peace with myself.

Shortly after this occasion, I was browsing in a gift store. Nothing appealed. But as I was leaving my eye caught sight of a statuette of the 'Laughing Buddha'. Instantly my monk came to mind. I purchased the Buddha and set him on a little altar in my bedroom. In times of turmoil since, I go to my altar, reflect on the Laughing Buddha and remember the great gift the monk gave me.

Marika Kohut   Victoria BC

Monica, Mother and Me

As the truck roared toward us, I clenched my teeth and forced myself to move away from Monica, far onto the shoulder of the road. Cringing and trembling, I was terrified. What if I couldn't resist the powerful urge to shove my best friend into its path?

Once the truck had passed by, I relaxed - not for long though, because three more vehicles were approaching. Who knows how many more there would be before we arrived at school. When we finally got there, I flung myself into the schoolyard, safe for now from carrying out this horrible deed. What kind of monster would have such thoughts – would want her best friend dead?! I was convinced there was no ten-year-old anywhere more evil than me.

I tried to think back – when had these sickening ideas first come to me? Why had I changed my mind about Monica – I used to love to spend time with her. When she wasn't at my house, I was at hers – up in our rooms, doing homework together, styling each other's hair, reading each other's diaries. Why did I resent her so much now? Others certainly didn't.

"Monica is so smart", my mother would say. "Look how nicely she walks. Why can't you stand up straight like she does. Doesn't she have beautiful hair. See how she takes care of her brothers – what a big help she is to her mom." I knew my mom would have traded me for Perfect Monica in a second. Who wouldn't if she had a choice?

One day I arrived home from school panicky and out of breath because it was getting even worse: I had come so close to pushing Monica into the traffic! My mother was standing at the sink peeling vegetables when I ran into the kitchen.

"You'd rather Monica was your daughter than me!" I heard my voice yelling.

My mother turned from her chore in surprise. "Of course not." She looked at me closely. "Is that what you think? Oh, I am so sorry." Tears glistened in her eyes and mine. "I love you very much. I'd never trade you for Monica or anyone, ever," she said, hugging me tight.

I felt wonderfully warm and light. The guilt and shame that had been torturing me was instantly and completely gone. In that moment, my best friend Monica's life was no longer in danger.

Judi Cumming   Vancouver BC

Out of the Blue!

To the casual observer, our life was probably pretty idyllic. My wife and I were blessed with a strong marriage; we had two bright, athletic children; we lived in a beautiful house; we had a summer cottage, and good jobs. But the happiness that should have been there wasn't. Perhaps it was mid-life crisis and a need for change. Was it that our mortgage and my endless commuting to and from a very dissatisfying job overshadowed the good things in my life? Maybe it was ingratitude for all that we had. Could it be that spirituality was missing from the list of blessings bestowed upon us? Might it be 'all of the above'?

It was a Sunday, and we were out exploring, as we often liked to do. Driving back to Oakville from a wonderful afternoon at the Elora Gorge, we came upon an 'open house' hosted by a realtor in Guelph. On impulse, we stopped and toured the house. Our interest was piqued, not so much by the house, but by the idea of how a major change in our lives might restore something that seemed to have gone missing. The remainder of our drive home was quiet and reflective.

No more than ten minutes after we arrived home, the telephone rang.

"Would you like to sell your house?" the real estate agent asked.

"But it is not for sale," I explained.

"If you are interested, I have a buyer!" was her reply.

It was as though Fate had looked us in the eye, and in that moment, issued a challenge. We seized the opportunity. Within three weeks we had sold the house, and chosen to return to our birthplace, London, Ontario. My wife had been offered a new job, and I began to lay plans for my new professional life.

The exhilaration of having one's prayers answered is wonderful and awe-inspiring. On the other hand, there is the fear of change and the unknown. Also, even anticipation of exciting new directions does not prevent sadness at leaving behind many fond friendships.

The changes we experienced were varied and significantly affected each of us. In the big picture, our willingness to take that risk showed us very clearly how our lives are shaped by our own choices and initiatives. Since that fateful day, we are more open to life's possibilities and freer to follow our hearts.

Terry Boucher   Peterborough ON

Warmth on a Wintry Day

At the age of 32, I suffered what I believe is the greatest loss in life - the sudden death of a spouse. My husband Paul, age 34, died of a heart attack while playing hockey.

It was late November, and I know that for several weeks I operated in shock, caring for my two young children and just trying to cope with daily life.

Blessed with good family and friends, I somehow knew that I could survive, and that I could look after my children. But what about Paul? Did he suffer? Was he okay? I needed some reassurance.

One chilly, grey morning in early December, I was backing the car out of the driveway. Suddenly I felt very warm and I experienced what I can only describe as a 'vision'. It was sunny and I saw Paul walking contentedly across a golf course. He was smiling and relaxed.

It was only a matter of seconds before I was back in the cold, gloomy car, but in that very real moment Paul gave me a message: 'I'm okay. I'm happy.'

That was all I needed to know.

Kathy Bissett   Ottawa ON

AHA!

Is the Latte Frothier on the Other Side?

It was 7:30 a.m. on a beautiful, crisp fall morning. I headed out the door for a morning run through my neighbourhood. I should begin by explaining that it's quite a nice neighbourhood, filled with big trees and hundred-year-old homes. I rent a single floor in one of these homes. I wouldn't be surprised if I were the only renter in an eight-block radius.

Most of the people in this area are young, well off couples with one or two beautiful children, all of whom are decked out in clothes from the GAP. I was a single, overtime-working, 27 year old renter. Let's put it this way, their lives looked a little more warm and cozy than mine.

Anyway, back to the run. As I made my way along my five kilometer route I saw a very pretty, well-dressed woman, about my age, coming towards me. Picture this if you will; she was pushing an expensive baby carriage that not only held a beautiful new born baby, but also cradled her grande latte from Starbucks in the convenient 'mommy-on-the-go' cup holder. She pushed the carriage with her right hand and in the left was the leash of her perfect, lit by the morning sun, golden retriever. All I could think as she approached was, 'God, I wish I had her life'.

As we passed, we both smiled and said good morning. In the moment that our eyes met and smiles were exchanged I got the overwhelming feeling that she was looking at me with her tired 'I'm the mother of a newborn, who at 7:00 a.m. has to scoop dog poop' eyes thinking, 'God, I wish I had her life'.

It was only at that moment, after 27 years of wanting the marriage/nice house/cute baby/obedient dog that I realized being a single renter actually allowed for unbelievable freedom. It dawned on me that there would be lots of time for all of those other things. If I enjoy what I have now, I'll enjoy what the future has to offer even more. Until then, the only responsibility I have to worry about is that rent cheque every month.

Danielle Krysa   Toronto ON

Sixty-Year Moment

Summer 1942

I am 26 years old and have been a registered nurse for two years. I have come home to Canada from Hartford, Wisconsin where I'd worked for a year and am now employed in the little hospital in the small town of Almonte, Ontario where I grew up. I am at loose ends. My immediate future seems fuzzy. There have been a couple of unsatisfactory relationships. I have even applied to join the RCAF with the idea of contributing my nursing skills to the war effort.

As I'm walking to the hospital for an afternoon shift, I stop at a street corner where I have stood hundreds of times before. But this time, I am distinctly aware of a voice saying to me, "Without me you can do nothing. With me you can conquer worlds." The message is like a flashing light, pointing to something - I'm not sure what. But I hang on to it – waiting.

I go back to Kingston, where I had taken my training, and continue nursing. I am a Roman Catholic and for many years, the thought of a religious vocation has been in my mind. But I believe I have cleverly evaded it by becoming a nurse and having a good time. At the end of November, my sister Margaret introduces me to a priest friend and we talk. At his gentle but persistent suggestion, I request to be admitted to the community of Religious Hospitallers of St. Joseph.

Winter 1943

With the words, 'With me you can conquer worlds' still in my ears, I become a somewhat reluctant postulant (the name given to those at the first level of training to become a nun).

Winter 1945

I make my final profession of vows of poverty, chastity and obedience and prepare to embark on a life of service to God and my fellow man. By now I am familiar enough with the Bible to recognize 'Without Me you can do nothing' from St. John's gospel and another version of 'With Me you can conquer worlds' in Paul's epistle to the Philippians: 'I can do all things in Him who strengthens me'. The meaning of the words resonates within me – I depend on God's presence in my life and strive to take my direction and strength from Him.

But through the ensuing decades, there is one tiny aspect of my message which puzzles me: why is 'worlds' pluralized?

Summer 2002

A member of my Book Club introduces me to an author who is new to me, Neil Bissoondath. I read his book, The Worlds Within Her. And now I KNOW! My 'worlds' are the circumstances, events and people who have led me to where I am today. My 'worlds' include all my relationships, trials and triumphs from the time of my birth, through school, nurse's training, religious vows, degree in Nursing Education, career of joyous service - teaching student nurses, novices and postulants, parishioners, and members of the community.

Sixty years later, the entire message of that mysterious moment is clear to me. These words which have been a beacon guiding my way, filling me with peace and gratitude, now shine with their full meaning.

Sister Mary Coderre, RHSJ
Amherstview ON

Collaborative Trust

The moment I realized that the value of any expended effort is in the process and not the outcome, I knew I had encountered an idea that could be generalized into all facets of living. Alas, if it were only that easy.

This experience came about as the result of a painting partnership with watercolorist Judi Cumming. We decided to collaborate as artists and began by taking turns painting on the same piece in an intuitive way. We did no initial sketching nor planning, and had no preconceived notion of the result.

It was not without some apprehension that I began this cooperative experiment. Artists can be very protective and possessive regarding their creations. I am no exception.

This apprehension vanished with the first brush stroke. I realized immediately that instead of creating a painting, we were responding to each other's marks on the paper in a rather surreal form of communication that was both energizing and inspiring.

This dialogue was also expanding in a professional way. Because she is a watercolorist, some of Judi's tools and techniques differed from those which I, as a calligraphic artist, was accustomed to using. Consequently, we both delighted in and learned from watching the other work and were often surprised by the new directions the collaboration inspired.

Our joint process resulted in two exhibitions of wide-ranging and diverse pieces but the real beauty in the experience was the release of personal investment in the outcome, and the joy in trusting the process as well as another human being.

Susan Nelson   Guelph ON

Holding Him

As I held him,
his small arms reached out,
away from me,
as if he were embracing
the beauty of the summer day.
I remember thinking -
take it.
It belongs to you.
The whole world belongs to you.

Holding him.
Breathing him in,
a new sensation -
a welcome one.
Adjusting - not just to his weight -
but to everything about him.
This relative stranger,
who had planted himself
so firmly in my heart -
after only eight days.

Blond, blue eyed
so beautiful.
Gary Christopher -
the names his birth-mother
gave him -
The names we chose to keep,
sensing that, at eleven months,
they were a part of him.

He was coming into my life
my soon-to-be adopted son.
And in that moment -
sharing the warmth
of the summer day -
with me holding him
and him reaching away,

I realized, and accepted,
that this would be my role.

To teach him well enough
for him to leave me.
To hold him tight,
until it was time
to let him go.

Margaret Coderre-Williams
Orleans, Ontario

Nothing is Real

I was about nine years old. It was early in the morning and I was just waking up. I opened my eyes and looked at the lump of my feet under the blanket, seen dimly in the glow of the pink-curtained window. The filtered sunlight fell on the creaky white wooden chair strewn with yesterday's clothes, the dark oak dresser that had belonged to my grandmother and was still protected by her hand-embroidered doilies, my softball mitt and grungy runners on the floor by the door.

The thought crystallizing in my consciousness applied equally to everything I saw – room, window, furniture, shoes, feet – and was at once mind-blowing and matter-of-fact: 'Aaaah – so that's how it works. None of this is real: we just make it up!'

Forty-six years later, it still rings true.

Judi Cumming   Vancouver BC

Napoleon WAS Here!

As a student, I went through elementary, high school, and even college quite successfully by being able to memorize facts and give back what was requested in essays and on exams. I didn't often question the reality of the information, but was quite trusting that what I heard in lectures or read in books was true.

At the age of 21, when I was in my first year teaching, my brother invited me to spend my spring break week in Paris, where he was living at the time. After my very first airplane flight, I confidently and in my best French directed my taxi driver to the Quartier Latin to meet Bob who had a busy schedule planned for me. As it was Sunday, our first stop was Mass at Notre Dame Cathedral.

I hardly remember anything of the service, which seemed to take place in a small corner of this immense church. However, as I sat there staring at the tall columns and at the worn marble floor, it suddenly struck me: this is the floor that Napoleon walked on, the very building where he crowned himself Emperor. In my mind's eye, it was 1804, the cathedral thronged with huge crowds of people, dressed in their finest, to witness the grand event. Hey, it's real! All that history I learned - it really did happen! This was my first encounter with solid physical proof of something I had only read about. I knew I wanted to see more.

Later in life, I have continued to travel, exploring great ancient sites – Roman ruins, the Pyramids, but still, my vivid realization that Sunday morning at Notre Dame remains my strongest proof that history lives.

Kathy Bissett   Ottawa ON

My Little Farmer

"He's a little farmer from Almonte but he is very nice and kind of cute."

This is the way my friend Jeannine described her fiancé's cousin, Larry. She often added, "I will have to introduce you." But she never did. She did, however, introduce me to his sister-in-law at a shower for a mutual friend. From that day, the women plotted our meeting. It was not easy because the 'little farmer' was working at his father's grocery store and did not come to the city very often. The opportunity arose when they learned that he was taking a holiday and would be in Ottawa on the Saturday night after his birthday. They planned a birthday party and I was invited as his blind date.

To break the ice, they arranged that we were to meet at the apartment of Jeannine and her husband before going to the party. I was waiting there apprehensively when Larry walked in. One look at his sparkling eyes, his cleft chin and his shy smile made me think he looked more like Alan Ladd than a farmer.

We talked for a little while and then all four of us walked the few blocks to the home of my date's brother and sister-in-law. I don't remember too much about the party except that everybody made me feel comfortable and I had a very good time. When it was time to leave, the two of us walked to my home, mostly in silence. I felt like an idiot for not being able to carry on a conversation. I felt sure that he would never want to see me again but I realize now that he was as shy as I was.

As we reached my front door, there was an awkward pause. I knew that I should say something like, 'Goodbye. Thank you for a beautiful evening', but I did not know how and besides I did not want to say goodbye. My date reached forward and with the crook of his index finger gently lifted my chin and kissed me softly on the lips.

The magic moment was broken when the front door burst open discharging a group of friends who had been playing cards with my mother. My hero, confused and embarrassed, beat a hasty retreat, leaving me to face the good-natured teasing of my mother's friends who had been told that I was on a blind date.

Sleep did not come easily that night but I awoke the next morning with a smile on my face. The magic of the moment was still there. On the way to church I overtook my aunt. I could not wait to share my good news. I told her with certainty in my voice and in my heart: "Last night, I met the man I am going to marry."

A year later I did marry him and forty-eight years after that, my little farmer and I are still very much in love.

Lucille Ranger Ottawa ON

Highway to Heaven?

The development of my hodgepodge beliefs started at an early age. I was born a very inquisitive child who had the privilege of a stay-at-home mom who, in turn, had the burden of the junior inquisition following her around the house all day:

"Alright, Mom, let's recap. How old is the world?"

"Millions and millions of years."

"Sure. And what was there before the world?"

"Just an empty universe, I guess."

"And before that?"

"Probably nothing."

"Okay, so where did everything come from?"

"Well, God created it all."

"Uh-huh, and who made God?"

"No one, God just always was."

"Right ..."

I was baptized in the Catholic Church and thereafter spent every Sunday, and any other day my mother deemed necessary, in a Catholic pew. And, while the image of an all-seeing, all-judging, lightning-bolt-slinging, bearded gentleman never convinced me, I did believe in *a* God or some higher power ...

And so it continued for years, seeing as spirituality is probably not the easiest thing to rationalize when you're the have-to-see-it-to-believe-it kind of person. For years, I had tried to let go of the unknowns, take it on faith, and find comfort in the rest. But rest, the inquisitive mind would not. So, it turned out that one summer afternoon when I was about twenty-one, on a stretch of two-lane highway in the middle of nowhere, I found my religion.

My older brother and I were a couple of hours into a road trip, when he asked me what I would do if someone handed me a sealed envelope containing an explanation of how the universe began. At last, a few simple answers to the biggest questions of our existence. Would I open it?

Before that moment, it had never really occurred to me how far our society had gotten without having any concrete proof of where it all started. We wake up in the morning; we make sure we arrive where we need to be on time. We learn how to make spreadsheets and get our whites whiter. We try to remember if the price of gas was cheaper six months ago, if the stove/iron/kettle is on. We stress over our families, jobs, relationships, tax audits, and the fact that some part of our anatomy used to be smaller/bigger/less creepy when we got our high school diploma. And as every one of these things in sequence becomes priority one, for all we know, our very existence could have started on a whim, and could end just the same way. And, in my mind, that's the greatest part.

"I wouldn't open it."

At some point, being the see-it-to-believe-it kind of person becomes a little dry and monotonous. If you remove all possibility of the unknown and fantastical from your life, where's the fun? It must have been amazing to live in a world where the sun, moon, wind, and the sea were all different gods and the first days of winter signaled the beginning of some morbid curse. Now, granted, the progress and discoveries made since that time ensure that I'm not compelled to sacrifice a sheep as soon as spring rolls around, but nevertheless, it must have been interesting not to know as much as we do today.

I won't go as far as saying that ignorance is bliss. Before I die and go on to -- well, who knows where -- I hope to learn as much as I can from the world's many belief systems. Each one of them has its own unique wealth of history and wisdom that I am drawn to more on a sociological than religious level.

More interestingly, though, for all their different views on how the world came to be, what all these religions share is the commitment that tomorrow, each one of us will try to be a better person than the one he is today. And, ultimately, if that is the goal towards which we are heading, does it really matter where we started?

For as insignificant and random as that moment on the highway might seem to someone else, I will never forget it. It set the results-driven, control-seeking person that I was, on the road to finding a comfort with the unknown -- whether in religion or anything else. It hasn't been the smoothest ride, but it promises to be easier tomorrow, and even more so the day after.

Amen to that.

Gregory Krysa   Toronto ON

Timeless Mindless

It was a bright sunny day in May, the kind you read about in stories. I had been living in 'res' for about nine months. No, not a 'res'ervation but a 'res'idence at a west coast university - a torrid, jumbled mass of gushing hormones and drink specials – wiped up periodically by custodians or undisciplined students on the wrong end of the worst reprimand imaginable in residence, the Incident Report.

There was nothing notable about that day; the morning passed as usual. I rounded up what cohorts I could find on my floor and went off to have my unappetizing bacon & powdered eggs breakfast.

As I walked out of our front foyer, befouled the night before by the gastric rejection of a large meat lovers' pizza and a bottle of blackberry vodka, there was a gleam around the concrete and gray stucco buildings that had not been there before.

I stepped forward, as if out of a glass bubble that had hovered around me all my years, now pinned stationary under the weight of my jettisoned fear and insecurities. At once I realized the grain of truth which spawned every established proverb and contradictory nugget of folk wisdom – 'Nobody's perfect', so I didn't have to be. 'There is nothing to fear but fear itself', so stop being afraid. 'Look before you leap', however 'He who hesitates is lost', so walk forward at half to three-quarter speed depending on your mood.

I thought about the knowledge within each of us that is entirely innate and unlearned and has been shared by every human at every point in time throughout history. I even understood the inspirational messages my mother had magnetized to our fridge during my childhood. 'What you perceive in others, you strengthen in yourself'. 'You reap what you sow'. 'Your thoughts make the world you see'. The golden rule had slapped me in the face.

But like all moments, this one was ephemeral, and soon those celestial baggage handlers had found and returned my emotional luggage. And yet, through the years since it happened, that sense of universal understanding now and then slips into my awareness, assuring me that it is not forgotten.

That day I had a double helping of eggs.

Cameron Cumming   Victoria BC

My Guardian Angel with Quills

It was 1947. After the war I was stranded in a little village at Lake Constance in the South of Germany, when the company I had been working for, a branch of the Askania Werke, Berlin, was taken over by the French. They dismantled our plant and took it - together with our leading ingenieurs - to France.

I longed to reunite with my parents who had settled in Hassfurt/Bavaria, which at the time was in 'American territory'. I had no problem buying a ticket and I boarded a train for Hassfurt but had no visa to cross from the French into the American zone. Many travellers had tried to 'jump' the border without a proper visa; most had failed. As our train approached the line, passengers without visas huddled together in little groups, exchanging ideas how to get across. Nothing seemed foolproof; the military had learned the hiding tricks real fast. I trusted that one way or the other help would arrive.

Someone asked me, "Do you have a visa?"

"No, I don't, I am just waiting for my guardian angel to supply me with one," I laughed, pretending not to be worried.

A young man approached me. "You seem more brave than convincing. Trust me, I can help." He pushed me into the next coach where nobody knew us, and revealed his 'foolproof' method to take me across the line. He showed me his credentials: a group visa between the French and the American zones for himself and 11 fellow students. They were members of a theater troupe, 'The Porcupines', organized to entertain both friend and foe with their satirical program.

"I can add your name to our list. Would you like to be a singer or a dancer?"

"I have a bit of experience in both fields," I replied without hesitation.

Billy Graf, student of law with the looks of Willy Heesters, a heartthrob of those years, added number 12, Margot Walter, (my maiden name) singer-dancer to the list. I could hardly believe it. Then in a flash I understood - Didn't I board the train trusting I would get the help I needed? Here it was!

The American soldiers entered our compartment, checked our passports and visa, gave us their 'OK' and a friendly nod, and we sailed safely into the American zone. Margot, the passenger with the least credibility, had found her guardian angel.

Margot Wawra   Abbotsford BC

INSIGHT

Washtub

If you open the windows of a room that has been closed for four hundred years, some people are bound to get dust in their eyes.

The Second Vatican Council, convoked by Pope John XXIII in 1961, threw open the ancient casements of the Catholic Church and the winds of change whirled through its entire structure. Rigid regulations, laid down in the sixteenth century to ensure uniformity, were replaced with more flexible guidelines. A small but very conspicuous change was to the Roman Missal. This book, written in Latin, contained the exact words to be prayed at Mass and instructions for the accompanying gestures to be used. One rubric even dictated the distance a priest's hand should travel while making the sign of the cross over the bread and wine! The prayers had been translated into the vernacular and the council encouraged bishops of the local churches to adapt the liturgy to be more compatible with culture and traditions of their people. Many Catholics, unable to distinguish between the dust and the structure, were deeply disturbed.

To help us clear the dust from our eyes, our pastor urged us to read the recently published Documents of Vatican II and he formed a study group to discuss them. Unfortunately, he was soon transferred to another parish. His successor did not have the same enthusiasm for church renewal. The study group was forgotten. The dust became thicker than ever. Traditionalists left in search of a Latin Mass. Reformers left for more progressive parishes. Others just left. The parish organizations floundered and even the choir was disbanded for lack of members.

This was a low point for me and I contemplated leaving too, but I kept coming back to Peter's words in

John 6:68, 'Lord to whom shall we go? You have the word of eternal life'.

It was at this time that a good friend invited me to attend a *Cursillo*, Spanish for 'a little course'. It was a weekend retreat with instructions, discussion, prayer and meditation. Each of us was assigned to a table of six to eight people and that group became our mutually supporting team. Mass was celebrated each day and the directors urged us to participate, responding to the prayers and singing the parts of the Mass. This joyful participation was new and exciting for us. On the last day, our team leader encouraged us to pray - aloud, for whatever we needed. This type of prayer was difficult for us who had learned formal prayers by rote and had kept our prayers of petition in the silence of our hearts.

I was very aware of the love given to me by my wife, children, family and friends. I knew in my mind that God loved me but my response to all this love seemed inadequate. I don't know why I chose those words or even if I was the one who chose them. I prayed, "Lord, teach me to love."

Sunday evening I returned home and later that night, after I'd been sleeping for some time, I had a vision, a dream - you name it. My heart was a large washtub made of darkly weathered wood. Into it a clear, colorless liquid was being poured - overflowing, immersing my whole body. It seemed sweet but it was not sticky like syrup. I became aware of the words: "This is all you will ever need and there is lots more where that came from." Although the word 'love' was not used, I know that the liquid was God's gift of love.

I woke up, overwhelmed with emotion, and began to cry tears of joy. I kissed my wife, saying from the depth of my being, "I love you, I love you." Was I talking to her? Or to God? I'm not sure - but I think I was talking to them both.

Not long afterward, I attended a Mass for *Cursillistas*. One of the readings included 2

Corinthians 4:7, "We are only the earthenware jars that hold this treasure."

Nothing about a wooden washtub but it was close enough for me.

Larry Coderre   Ottawa ON

Man the Protector

During the Second World War I worked as a payroll clerk for the Askania company in Berlin, manufacturer of precision instruments for aeroplanes. In 1943, I was transferred to a newly opened branch, the Geraetewerk Pommern, to operate their payroll office. I was happy to get away from the bomb attacks on Berlin, not knowing what was awaiting me in Kluetzow/Pomerania.

On a sunny October Day in 1944, the sirens were screeching their warning signal that British bombers were on their way. We were used to this, and usually just left the grounds to seek shelter away from our workplace. Often we went to a nearby forest, sitting on the grass, singing, happy that we had a break from the dull 12-hour working day. Often, we watched the black birds flying south, pushing away warning thoughts that they did not carry mail or food but deadly bombs.

This October 6, I had a feeling of doom that tore me away from my singing comrades. I ran as fast as I could down the highway. That was my luck. Only moments later, the falling bombs were shredding some of my friends to pieces. I heard bullets hitting the ground to my left and to my right. The flyers were aiming at this tiny target in a red and green summer dress. I rolled into a ditch, face down, pressing my fingers into my ears. The earth trembled as the bombs leveled the factories and our homes.

Suddenly, something heavy crushed my body. What was it? My God, I did not want to die, I was only 19 years old! I just tried to breathe deeply and think of nothing. Then I noticed that I was not breathing alone. When the attack finally stopped, the weight lifted. I turned around and looked into the face of the young German soldier who had protected me with his own body. His dirt-colored uniform had melded with the earth and mercifully covered my colourful dress, the target of my shooters. My life was spared by this soldier's selfless act of bravery.

"You could have been hit and died! Were you not afraid?" I asked my guardian angel.

"I am a soldier, and I see it as my duty to protect women from the wrath of war," he answered matter-of-factly.

We said good-bye and wished each other well. He went his way; I went mine, never to see each other again.

From that time, the image of 'man, the protector' became a very important part of my life. The kind, earth-smeared face of the unknown soldier and his warm, shielding body that spared my life is an image that lives in me to this day. Later, when in the course of war I faced plundering Russian forces and then French invaders with their marauding Moroccan soldiers, I just opened the memory book of my soul and trusted that there might be more protecting men in this world. There were.

Margot Wawra   Abbotsford BC

Demons

Until I was in my late thirties, I remembered very few of my dreams – two that were striking from my childhood and after that only occasional fragments drifting by as I awoke or startling me into consciousness in the middle of the night.

In the 1980's, there was a resurgence of mainstream interest in dreams. The more books and television programs I saw on the subject, the more interested I became. Finally, I signed up for a week-long workshop in the hope of discovering more about the dreaming process and why so many of my dreams remained hidden from me.

The facilitator told us that people do, indeed, dream daily and advised us 'to make a conscious effort as you fall asleep, to remind yourselves to remember your dreams'. He spoke impressively of the important messages contained in dreams, urging us to play close attention to them because 'an unexamined dream is like an unopened letter'.

During the workshop week, I began to practice the instructor's advice and - voila! I remembered - not every day and sometimes only fragments, but still, I found my success rate amazing.

When I returned home to my normal routine, the process continued to work. I kept a dream journal on my bed table (another suggestion from the course) and if I woke during the night in mid-dream, I wrote it down. A few times I tried waiting until morning only to find that the content of the dream, so vibrant and real at the time, had evaporated completely in the light of day.

One such middle of the night experience was unique. I awoke from a sound sleep with an awareness of a soft, blue-green shining accompanied by a tremendous sense of comfort and well-being. Though wordless and imageless, the message was very clear - even in my somnolent state I remember thinking: 'I know that – of course it's true'. As I was drifting back to sleep, a command came through accompanied by a tingling on my skin like static electricity: 'Write it down!'

I was tired and annoyed – why was it necessary to record something so obvious?! Besides, how would I express it? My feeble mental reply: 'No words'. Instantly a translucent, multicolor ribbon of words floated past. I groped in the dark for pen and notebook and copied the words from the banner.

The next morning I recalled perfectly waking in the turquoise light, recognizing the truth of the message, the urgent directive to write it down and the ribbon of words. But I had not the slightest idea what those words had been. I lay there, racking my brain for a few seconds, before it dawned on me to check the notebook! Six barely legible words wobbled across the page:

Demons exist only as manufactured reality

Judi Cumming   Vancouver BC

Anxiety

This is a poem I wrote to my wife Elaine shortly after we found out she was pregnant for our first child some 29 years ago. I have thought about it over the years but knew nothing of its whereabouts. Recently, as I was looking unsuccessfully for something else, lo and behold, it suddenly appeared.

As I read it, I found myself reliving the intense feelings that stirred me then. The excitement was there and the happiness of knowing we were bringing a new person into the world – mixed with the dread of such an awesome responsibility.

As I wrote these lines so many years ago, the power of our shared love and Elaine's capacity to be a wonderful mother became very clear to me. In that moment, I knew we had nothing to fear.

It's a bit corny, but it came from the heart.

Because of our love,
   You didst conceive.
Because of our love,
   A child will be born.
Born into a world
   Riddled with suffering and pain
And corruption and hate
   But, because of our love,
This child will experience
   Only the joys of life:
Happiness and love.

   Because of you.

Pat Coderre   Kingston ON

Internal Youth

I looked at the display of little boxes at Wal-Mart, gliding my fingers over the smooth checkered surface, contemplating how I could use them to organize odds and ends, fashion jewelry, buttons and bows.

"Buying things for going back to school?" asked a kindly voice, belonging to a gentleman who had some time for a friendly chat.

"Old women have use for these boxes too," I remarked, "to bring order into little bits and pieces."

"Good show, lady," the man said, "but please leave the 'old woman' out of the picture. You are no old woman, remember this ..."

It sounded different than my teacher's comments at my regular gym sessions: "This exercise is good for old people like you." Who needs a steady reminder of the fleeting years that bring wrinkles, aches and pains?

The casual exchange with this stranger had put a smile on my face, a spring in my step and a song in my heart – signs of the vitality undiminished inside me. To this day his words reverberate in my soul, "You are no old woman, remember this..."

Margot Wawra   Abbotsford BC

A Moment of Truth

I have always been a 'water-baby'. I learned to swim when I was very young and loved to play in the water. Water was my friend, I learned very early not to fear it; but it also seems that I did not learn to respect it.

When I was 21 I had a marvelous summer job with the Weather bureau. I was working at the construction site of the nuclear power station at Bruce Point on Lake Huron. I was one of four students at the site, taking weather measurements and water samples for the government.

On a beautiful warm summer day three of us were taking advantage of a break in the work routine, playing in the water at what was going to be the outlet channel for the reactors' coolant water. At this time though, it was just a 20-foot wide channel cut 20 feet deep into the flat rocks of the shore of the lake. One of the students was a chubby fellow (let me call him Corky) for he could float like a cork but, strangely enough, could not swim. We were having fun, carefree in the water, with no thought that within a few moments at least two lives would be at risk.

We were on the far side of the channel from our cabin. As we were barefoot and the broken rocks at the site were painful to walk on, I offered to tow Corky across the channel to save him the walk. He readily agreed and I started to tow him across the channel, swimming on my back, guiding him along with one of my hands under his shoulder as he floated on his back. I do not know exactly what happened next, perhaps a splash of water went into Corky's face, but whatever triggered it, he panicked and began to scramble all over me. He climbed up my body and suddenly I found myself underwater with Corky's legs locked tightly around my neck. He was thrashing about wildly, although his head was well above water. My situation was much more dire.

I kicked and stroked the water as hard as I could to try to get some air. It was impossible. He was too heavy. After what seemed an eternity I realized that it was futile. With Corky on my back I would never get high enough in the water to breathe. What's worse I was wasting what little strength, and air, I had left.

Time seemed to slow to a snail's pace as I thought, 'What can I do? If he drowns, it will be my fault!' I knew I too would drown and likely before him. He was a floater; he was in no real danger, but I was underwater and out of breath. An icy calmness seized me. I realized at that moment, with utmost certainty, I was not going to die; but, I had to work out what I could do to save Corky and myself.

My mind was working clearly and calmly, almost independent of myself. I decided that my only option was to try to pull him under with me. As it was, I was his point of safety. As long as I was holding him up, he was safe. So I figured if Corky thought I was pulling him down, he might let go of me before his head went under water too. I reverse-stroked with my arms, to try to get as deep as possible. My legs were of no use, trying to get down, so it was all arm swimming.

After an agonizingly long moment he released my head from his legs. With my last vestiges of strength I swam away from him, staying underwater as long as I could. Our very lives depended on me getting a precious breath of air before he could grab me again.

I surfaced about ten feet from where he was still in a panic, splashing frantically. I took a few deep breaths and slowly swam back towards him wondering what to do. The situation I had just escaped could easily repeat. I considered knocking him unconscious, but realized I was hardly likely to connect with enough force to do more than panic him further. I swam into position behind him, put one hand under his chin and in a firm voice said, "Calm down!" Miraculously, he quieted immediately. I cannot describe the relief I felt as he lay back quietly on the water and I cautiously towed him back to the point where we had started.

Since that moment, I have had the deep-down confidence of knowing that if I am ever thrown into a difficult situation, I will not panic. I will coolly appraise the situation and take whatever action is necessary. But, I am equally convinced that I will never again take for granted the danger that water can bring. I am still a 'water-baby', but a much wiser one for this experience.

Bill Coderre   Ottawa, Ontario

When To Say Good Bye

My lack of skill with houseplants is well known among family and friends. I have received many plants as gifts over the years, none of which survived long after taking up residency with me. I have never purchased a houseplant. "How could I be so inept?" I ask myself, especially when I visit homes where the foliage and blossoms flourish.

Imagine my shock when, two years ago, my children gave me a houseplant for Mother's Day. In response to my look of horror my son hugged me and suggested:

"Take up the challenge, Mom. Just do your best."

Today that hearty plant stands tall and beautiful, although totally green. I have even rooted and potted slips!

In my recently acquired leisure time since retiring, I decided to do some research on how I might help my object of pride produce the pretty flowers it bore when I received it. I began my search at the library. Although I have yet to find the solution to my query I did read a chapter in one of the books, which I felt may have been written 'to me'.

As I read 'When To Say Good Bye' I could feel a great burden being lifted from my shoulders. I learned that, not only should many houseplants not be expected to live forever, but also it is not unusual for many to survive only a year or less. I concluded, therefore, that I should not feel guilty returning to the earth a plant, which must be put in its final resting place despite my attempt to meet all its needs.

So now, I am free to rejoice in the success I have had and continue in my quest for blooms among my beautiful green leaves.

Barbara Purdy   Elgin ON

Don't Ask Why

My early childhood was a happy one. We were very poor and when I was born we lived in one room at the back of my father's butcher shop. My mother had severe back problems but to me that only meant that she had more time to read me stories and teach me to knit and embroider.

Shortly after my brother was born, when I was not quite five, my world was turned upside down. It wasn't just that I had a sibling to contend with. One morning my mother's friend arrived and bundled my mother in her winter coat over her nightgown and led her through the Winnipeg winter snow piles to a taxi.

She spent the next two months in a psychiatric ward. Occasionally, I was taken to the hospital so I could stand outside and wave to my dear mother who waved back from inside the heavily barred windows.

Today, I think my mother probably would be diagnosed with postpartum depression. I don't know what the diagnosis was back then but she was treated with electric shock therapy. Over the 20 years that followed there were recurring 'break downs', suicide attempts and hospitalization. My father, each time, would go on and on asking, pleading, "Why is this happening to me?"

I remember very clearly a situation that happened when I was in my early teens. My father was anguished and desperate. He sat at the table with his head in his hands begging to know why. As I stood at the doorway confounded by his distress, a powerful idea played in my mind: What difference would it make if there was an answer?

Little did I know that my 'enlightenment' would provide me with the basis of coping skills to see me through my life's crises. It keeps me looking forward and not back. To me, to ask ' Why is this happening to me?' for more than a passing moment is to be 'stuck' and 'not coping'.

This way of looking at things helped me when my ten-year-old daughter, Brenda, was diagnosed with a fatal brain disease. She was hospitalized for 18 months before she died. During her illness, Ruth, my mother-in-law, was diagnosed with bowel cancer and died. Six months after our daughter's death, my husband Tom, age 45, was diagnosed with terminal stomach cancer and died six months after that.

Throughout these incredibly difficult years I often reflected, "What difference would it make if I knew why this happened to me?" It had happened, was happening, and I had to do the very best I could to accept it and live with it.

Not questioning why didn't prevent the pain and heartbreak but it did help me to see the tiny speck of light at the end of that very dark tunnel.

Gina Hartley   Abbotsford BC

September 11 - Hard Lesson in Priorities

Some people's 'moments of clarity' are very personal - others are shared. My moment was probably experienced by many, in one way or another, because it was a direct result of the events of September 11, 2001. My moment occurred at approximately 8:30 p.m. on that day.

Earlier that day, as the entire office was huddled around the TV, our way of life was changing before our very eyes. Just moments after the first tower of the World Trade Center fell, the Creative Director of our agency made an announcement that the studio was closing so that everybody could go home and be with their loved ones. I decided to stay, at least for a few more hours, to finish a stationery package I was working on for a sporting goods manufacturer.

Don't get me wrong, I knew the events that were taking place south of the border were tragic. But I suppose I also thought the terrorist attacks were just going to be a blip on the radar. I had no idea they were going to have such a rippling effect – an impact that we are still feeling today, two years later.

It wasn't until that evening that my moment of clarity occurred. It happened while my girlfriend and I sat on the couch watching George W address congress and the US citizens. When Bush looked up from his notes and said in a strong and unforgettable voice, "You are either with us...or you are with the terrorists", a chill went up my spine. He was demanding that the nations of the world choose sides, and if they weren't 'with the good guys' they would feel the wrath of the United States of America.

Fear gripped me as I wondered how far he would go. Would the US declare war on countries based on suspicion and emotion? Would there be a roundup of all suspected ethnic groups reminiscent of

Germany in the late 1930's? It sounds a little crazy now, but at the time it seemed like anything was possible.

Something was triggered inside me. I realized with sudden clearness how I had been caught up in the unimportant things. The career, which had defined my life, now seemed trivial and inconsequential.

Before September 11th, I believed my work was the most important thing in life. I guess it was partially arrogance and partially the environment surrounding me. Graphic design can be a very superficial world that judges mainly on image. Think of it, at the same time as people were throwing their helpless bodies off the 110th floor of the World Trade Center, I was meticulously fixing the spacing between the numbers on somebody's business card.

If that wasn't bad enough, the company whose work I was doing as the terrorist attacks occurred, announced the very next day that they had bought a manufacturer of American flags. I thought I was going to be sick - the very idea of trying to capitalize on the death of thousands was utterly revolting.

As time went on and the healing process was beginning, I started to get very introspective. Had I, up to that point, wasted my life in a career that helped rich companies become richer? Was I playing any sort of positive role in society? It was a pretty dark place I have to tell you.

Now that the dust has settled somewhat, I have made some changes in my life. The list below shows my priorities before September 11th and my priorities now. I may not be able to change the world, but I may be able to change myself.

Life Priorities Before September 11th

1) Career
2) Family and Friends

3) Become a Rock Star

Life Priorities After September 11th

1) Family and Friends
2) Become a Better Person
3) Become a Rock Star

Consider it a work in progress.

Dave Watson   Toronto ON

My New Coat

Let me tell you of an episode that is etched in my memory and which is probably typical of the happenings in many families during the Great Depression. In 1932, the year I turned eleven, Mom and I both needed spring coats and the necessary money had been painstakingly saved. We went down to the local clothing store, Laidlaw's, and tried on coats for me. Mom finally settled on a mustard-coloured tweed coat, which I abhorred, but the price was right - five dollars. The one I had my heart set on was a beautiful midnight blue with a crepe-de-chine scarf in a lighter blue. When Mom pointed out that she could not afford to pay the ten dollars that it cost if she were to buy a coat for herself too, I couldn't say much.

Steeped in the misery of having to wear that horrible mustard-coloured coat, I did not notice that Mom seemed to be extra fussy about all the coats she tried on. She finally decided that she would have to look elsewhere. It was late so she put it off until the next day and we went home with me carrying, reluctantly, the box with my new coat.

When Dad came home for supper I still had not opened the box. I just did not want to look at that coat again. When Mom insisted that I show Dad my new coat, I finally opened the box and there, in all its splendour, was the blue coat! I was in seventh heaven and it wasn't until weeks later that I realized that Mom was still wearing her shabby old coat. She insisted that she just had not found one to fit. I don't think I ever told her how much I appreciated what she'd done and how long I have remembered it. I still get a lump in my throat thinking about it.

This recognition of the depth of my mother's love for me was a changing point in my life. Not only did it influence the way I spoke to my Mom through my teens but, more than that, it also affected my dealings with my own children as they reached those difficult years. Whenever we held opposing views, the impact of the coat episode reminded me of my teenage self and helped me choose my words more carefully. That way, we were usually able to avoid the shouting arguments that many of my friends considered normal conversations with their teenagers.

Thanks Mom.

Anita Coderre   Ottawa ON

The Empty Room

At first, I thought I had walked into the wrong room. I'd never before seen this room empty. Not once in three years of hospice visiting.

Strange how each person made the room seem somewhat different. The last several weeks it had taken on a whole new atmosphere...it had gone from a sad place of dying to this joyful place of departure ... the platform, Sylvia said, from which she would step into the arms of Jesus.

Recently, Edith had come to share the room with Sylvia. Before her had been other roommates, but none with the brightness of Edith.

Edith and Sylvia – together by chance, by fate? reached out to each other, held hands as doctors probed, and nurses nursed, shared secrets and fears. There was no time to waste.

Sylvia had seen her mother waiting - in the corner of the room in the shadows at first and then lit up so radiantly, her arms reaching out, her face smiling.

Strangely, Edith too experienced a supernatural maternal visit, but with a different message. Her mother said that Edith's work was not yet done; there were people who needed her still.

Edith would sometimes lie awake and listen to Sylvia's breathing, praying for her, praying that her time would not be much longer. She knew Sylvia was tiring of this sickly lingering and that she was unafraid, at peace, ready now.

They had agreed that, although they didn't have nearly all the answers, they felt the peace and joy of a loving heavenly Father, and trusted He had prepared for them a place in heaven.

And so, one day Sylvia was there and the next she was sleeping, perpetually sleeping... comatose maybe, no one ever really said. Edith's dear new friend was there, beside her in the next bed, but gone.

103

Still each night she continued to read aloud from the New Testament, feeling that somewhere Sylvia was listening.

They hadn't really said good-bye. They had said goodnight though, the night before, thanking each other as they did, for another wonderful day of laughter.

Soon after, as Sylvia was no doubt settling nicely in to her place in heaven, Edith's mother must have paid her another visit, to say, "Come my child, it is time".

As I stood in the empty room, the deep caring the two women shared in their last days poured its warmth over me. From that gentle, powerful feeling came the knowledge that all is well, that love prevails, that friendship prevails - that death is a beginning.

Cynthia Lee-Strawford Peachland BC

ONENESS

Insight into Light

On a beautiful summer day I sat outside the Granville Island Public Market in Vancouver, enjoying the sunshine, the light on the water and my morning coffee. The sounds of laughter, children playing, and flute music were soft in the background; it seemed a feeling of quiet contentment had settled on all of us sharing this place.

As I looked at the people who surrounded me - a child feeding the pigeons, friends walking by, chatting - I began to notice that where I had seen only physical bodies moments earlier, I was now seeing lights - lights so bright that the bodies were barely discernable in the background. As I stared in amazement, I could see that these 'lights' were joined and each one appeared equal in its intensity and brightness, unlike the very different bodies in the background. I felt overwhelmed by a feeling of love and connectedness with these people.

Once I recovered from the initial 'wow', I thought to myself, OK, so THIS is what it means when it is said that we are all Light, we are all equal and all of life is interconnected. I thought I already knew that, but seeing it so graphically presented before my eyes made it a very real knowing - something I understood in my heart not just my mind. Although this way of seeing lasted only a minute at the most, it is imprinted on my heart as a gift which has helped me immensely in my life.

Whenever I'm tempted to make judgements about people, based on appearances, abilities or situations, I remember that magical moment - the shimmering water, the sunshine and our very real connection to each other with light and with love. I remember that what I see physically in front of me as 'the truth' is not the whole reality - not even close!

Kate Miller   North Saanich BC

The Birthday Yogi

That morning I took my usual position seated on the living-room sofa, focused on my breath and began to calm my mind for meditation. However, this time was different from the usual because I had been reading about out-of-body experience and had decided to try it. I wasn't contemplating anything big, like astral travel for instance; I just wanted to exit my body and hover around near the ceiling for a while! I held this request in my mind – nothing happened. I was aware only of sitting on the couch, breathing and becoming increasingly frustrated that I was unable to take even this tiny first step out of my body. After about an hour, I gave up and went about my usual household chores.

At noon, four close friends showed up at the door to take me out for a fortieth birthday lunch, or so they told me. On the way to the restaurant, we turned onto a quiet residential street that I didn't recognize and stopped in front of one of the houses.

They had made an appointment for me with a psychic! This was new for me - but something I'd been wanting to try.

I was introduced to Dorothy, who was warm, friendly and looked like everyone's favorite aunt. We made ourselves comfortable in the living room while my friends adjourned to the family room downstairs. She explained that she didn't do readings herself, but rather channeled a yogi who spoke through her. Without further ado, she looked me in the eyes, smiled and said:

"He says it is not necessary for you to leave your body."

I was shaken – my heart was pounding. How could she/he possibly know this? I had told no one about it. I was even somewhat embarrassed by the whole experience. She went on, "Does this make sense to you?"

"Yes." I could only manage a whisper.

Luckily, our session was being taped because I barely heard the rest of what she said. I was overwhelmed by the astounding yet terrifying possibility that my mind is not private! If Dorothy's yogi knows what I'm thinking, who else does? Do I now have to be careful to 'think before I think'? Does it work both ways - can I access the minds of others?

Everyone talks about the idea that there is an awful lot going on that we don't perceive. My visit with Dorothy made that idea very real for me - made me realize how limited my awareness is. Ever since, I have been trying to find ways to expand it.

Judi Cumming   Vancouver BC

I Belong to the Earth

A lovely beach in Western Australia. I lie down in the shade of a carved rock, enjoying the tranquility, the pristine beauty, the perfect rhythm of the waves. Nobody around for miles. I fall asleep.

I wake up with the strong sense of a presence close by: an enormous sea lion is lying so near I could roll twice and touch him. My first thought is, he must be dead, washed up on the beach. But before I make a move he suddenly lifts his head and looks at me - a few seconds of hesitation then he relaxes and goes back to sleep. He accepts me; I am not a threat.

He is exhausted - must have been out at sea feeding for days. I watch his massive, shiny body heave with each breath; I share his weariness.

During my travels across Australia I have been reading and enquiring about the beliefs of the Aboriginals, trying to feel and understand their connection to the earth.

As I lie peacefully so close to this huge creature, in the core of my being I know: I belong to the earth, just a particle yet valuable, no more no less than the sea, the sun, the rock and the sea lion.

Since then my thoughts go back often to that beach; the need to recapture that moment of total balance and harmony is strong. It inspires me to wonder: could that be what dying is - a peaceful return to the earth where we belong?

Catherine Poupard   Summerland BC

The Kiss

One August evening, my future husband Dan and I were strolling in Queen Elizabeth Park in Vancouver. Dubbed Little Mountain by the locals, its walking paths by beautiful gardens and ponds up to a tumbling waterfall made it one of our very favorite spots. The sun had set, leaving the deep, radiant blue of twilight settling on the grassy hills and gigantic firs, cedars and hemlocks surrounding us. The sweet summer air was damp with impending dew.

Enjoying the shelter of the ancient conifers, we stopped beside a solitary hemlock with spiky, droopy branches that reminded us of a crotchety spinster. On one of our previous visits we had given her a name. "How are you, Edith?" I called. As usual, she returned my greeting with silent disdain, turning her branches away in the breeze.

Happily, Dan was friendlier. He leaned down to kiss me, as he often did. But this time was like no other. Incredibly, I shifted into everything around me – 'Edith' and the other trees, earth, cliffs, waterfall, the lover who held me – we were all one. In a moment of pure freedom, I was the luminous purple of the sky, the healing fragrance of the soil, the comforting mass of the mountain, the passionate heart of the man I loved. No sparrow, squirrel, water lily, snail, waft of air nor grain of sand was left out – they were me; I was them.

Although the amazing 'shift' has not yet recurred in the many years since it happened, its power stays with me. I feel so grateful for that glimpse of a different, glorious way to experience the world: a door opened for me that can never be closed.

Judi Cumming   Vancouver BC

Going for the 'Gold'

While I have always been active and involved in sports, I am highly average. No, not 'high average' more like, 'middle of the road, I'd better be doing this for myself because nobody else is going to be impressed average'.

In about 1985 I decided I should start jogging. That wouldn't be so surprising except that near the end of my active soccer career (1965), playing for the University of British Columbia, I had jammed my left knee so badly that I had never been able to jog without experiencing major pain after about a mile. I decided that if I could jog for a mile before it hurt, I would jog for a mile. That is how my later life running career began. To date, I have run everything from 5K's to marathons.

My favorite form of running is the road relay. It all started with Don, my good friend and family doctor, who was all excited about a special event that was being developed as part of the Expo '86 extravaganza: the Okanagan Express Relay. This little jaunt started in Vancouver from just outside the Eastern Expo gates and traveled some 450 km to Summerland, just north of Penticton. Upon learning of my exercise plan, it was Dr. Don who got me into the relay for the first time.

I enjoyed myself so much that when the second Okanagan Express Relay was taking shape in 1987, I signed up to do it again. The event takes place over a couple of days with 26 team members each running legs of 10-29 km, depending on the terrain. I was part of the Summerland Roadrunners, as was Don. We weren't good enough to beat the top competitors but we could hold our own with the locals.

As the race unfolded, we found ourselves very evenly matched with two other teams and had been duelling with them from the beginning. Ernie, one of our better and more determined runners was to take the last leg of the relay. When he started for the finish line in Summerland, both our rivals were ahead of us, one by just a little and the other by a lot. Ernie set his sights on the nearest team, relentlessly tracking them down and passing their runner with just 5 km to go. From the support vehicles we hooted and cheered like mad, thinking that this pass was our final glory moment of the race.

But then, the scout vehicle returned to report the other rival team was not very far ahead on the curving lakeshore road. Anyone who knows the Okanagan and Highway 97 North, is familiar with the formidable 'Summerland hill'. From the bottom of that hill, we could see our quarry about halfway up. Their runner was clearly struggling. It was all Ernie needed. He pounded up the hill, closing the distance with every stride, seeming not to notice he was on one of the longest, steepest climbs on the route. Near the crest of the hill and about 2 km from the finish, our man was within a few meters of his rival. As he passed, we all screamed and cheered. Yes, for him of course, but surprisingly, also for our rival runner because that was what this kind of race was about. Shouts of 'Come on – you can do it – you're almost there!' were for both.

We turned onto town streets and everybody but the drivers leaped out of the vehicles and got behind our man as we raced toward the finish at the center of town. Striding out those last few blocks as a team, I suddenly understood why the relay is my favorite kind of running. Of course, our anchor runner was going to cross the finish line ahead of the two teams he had passed in the last of the 26 legs that made up the race, but he didn't do that by himself. Each of the 26 members of our team (and every other team, for that matter) was part of what played out in the last meter of that race. (After some 37 hours 27 minutes and 47 seconds of non-stop competition, the three teams of this story crossed the line in less than one minute.)

As I passed under the finish banner on the heels of our official runner, the feeling of oneness with that group was one of the most powerful feelings you could imagine. There was also a clear sense that even though the team was like a living entity in its own right, every runner, including me, was an equally indispensable part of it.

I have run a number of relays since then. All have been special and filled with the same spirit, but it was that one moment as we surged over the line together that defined everything. The feeling of 'and this is what it is all about' has never been stronger or more brilliantly clear for me. I knew without question that every runner on every team had 'gone for the gold' and got it in their own personal way on that sunny summer Sunday in the Okanagan.

Dan Cumming   Vancouver, BC

Love, Dad

Five days after my father died, I was alone on the eight-hour drive from my parents' village of Nakusp in the Columbia River valley of British Columbia to my home, the city of Abbotsford in the Fraser Valley, when I began to enter an altered state of consciousness. It grew slowly but steadily from an awareness of the beauty and perfection of the natural world around me to an experience of ecstasy and unity with the universe itself. I found myself driving seamlessly with the car and the road and myself being one entity - every gear shift and every curve were executed perfectly and as time passed, without my conscious effort at all. The car was an old Volvo P1800 that required attention to make it operate smoothly at the best of times so this was quite extraordinary.

My conscious awareness expanded and encompassed the natural world around me from horizon to horizon. I was vast - I was in complete unity with the sky, the lake, the earth. I felt sure that could I but remove a filmy veil from my eyes, the answers to the why's of life would be known. My body was there but I wasn't aware of its weight or pressure or physicality - I was in my head, my mind, my consciousness.

Then messages started coming into my awareness - one after another - but not rapidly. Each one waited until the preceding one was integrated. They began with, 'Do not be afraid'. Then, 'I am okay. All is well.' So I understood that even though there was no voice, Dad was talking to me. 'Know that you are deeply loved' permeated my being and carried me for miles. 'Take care of your fellow time travelers' came with images of teapots and hands holding cups of tea. Then came 'No ego: You are all brothers and sisters; Your time here is very brief. Go gently: People do the best they can. Laugh, dance, sing, play, work (in that highly significant order with work coming at the end in direct contrast to how I was raised); Do your best; Do not contribute to planetary suffering.'

This is a drive that I normally find tiring but I arrived home as fresh and clear as when the journey began. My feet barely touched the ground as I unloaded the car. I was in a state of ecstasy - certainly beyond joy or peace. The world looked perfect to me just as it was - without my intervention - without my tidying things up - without my help - it was in fact okay just as it was.

This state of bliss lasted for at least 48 hours with a slow re-entry into the everyday plane of reality. I had been aware from the very first message that this was all coming from Dad, although there was no voice. These mind messages were clearly his way of reaching out to try to help me come to terms with his death and with the meaning of life and how best to live it.

Since that amazing drive, now and then my father still finds ways, after death, to give me the roadmap that he tried so hard to give me in life. What else is there to know?

Olwyn Irving   Abbotsford BC

INDEX OF AUTHORS

Bissett, Kathy ... 33, 62, 72
Boucher, Pam ... 14
Boucher, Terry ... 60
Chantler, Neil ... 51
Coderre, Anita ... 101
Coderre, Bill ... 92
Coderre, Dave ... 31
Coderre, Larry ... 15, 83
Coderre, Mary ... 28, 66
Coderre, Nita Michelle ... 26
Coderre, Pat ... 90
Coderre-Williams, Margaret ... 11, 69
Cumming, Cameron ... 78
Cumming, Dan ... 37, 111
Cumming, Janna ... 54
Cumming, Judi ... 20, 55, 58, 71, 88, 107, 110
Emery, Sarah ... 26
Emery, Stephen ... 39
Hartley, Gina ... 96
Irving, Olwyn ... 114
Kohut, Marika ... 40, 56
Krysa, Danielle ... 49, 64
Krysa, Gregory ... 75
Lee-Strawford, Cynthia ... 42, 103
Looby, Mary Elizabeth ... 22
Miller, Judy ... 24
Miller, Kate ... 106
Nelson, Susan ... 68
Oxford, Jeffrey S. ... 17
Poupard, Catherine ... 109
Purdy, Barbara ... 95
Ranger, Lucille ... 73
Stokholm, Allison ... 44
Watson, Dave ... 98
Wawra, Margot ... 35, 80, 86, 91

ISBN 141201753-X